When "I Love You" Turns Violent

When "I Love You" Turns Violent

Recognizing and Confronting Dangerous Relationships

Revised and Expanded Edition

Scott A. Johnson

New Horizon Press
Far Hills, New Jersey

Copyright Acknowledgements

The author and publisher gratefully acknowledge permission to use the following materials:

Figure 1 is adapted from the *Power and Control Wheel, Domestic Abuse Intervention Project*, Duluth, MN. Used with permission.

Portions of Appendix VI are adapted from material by the Family Violence Network, Lake Elmo, MN. Used with permission.

Johnson, Scott A.
When "I Love You" Turns Violent: Recognizing and confronting dangerous relationships
Revised and Expanded Edition

Cover Design: Andrea Rotondi
Interior Design: Susan M. Sanderson

Library of Congress Control Number: 2004118082

ISBN: 0-88282-262-4
New Horizon Press

Manufactured in Canada

2009   2008   2007   2006   2005 / 5   4   3   2   1

Table of Contents

Figures

Author's Note

This book is based on extensive personal interviews with men and women, experience counseling couples and a thorough study of the available literature. Fictitious identities and names have been given to characters in this book in order to protect privacy. Some characters may be composites. For the purposes of simplifying usage, the pronouns *he* and *she* are sometimes used interchangeably.

Acknowledgments

I would like to thank the following people:

Pat and George Johnson, my parents, for all of the support they provided; Rosalie Clark, Professor at Augsburg College, for getting me interested in the relationship violence field; DeeAnn Kreatz-Rosen and Kathy Kreatz, for their support, talents, contributions and friendship.

I would like to thank my colleagues for their feedback and contributions: Dr. Michael L. Cesta, M.D.; Brian L. Nelson, M.Div., M.A., L.P.; Barb Thorsen, R.N., M.S., L.A.D.C.; William Cohen, M.S., M.Div., L.I.C.S.W., L.P.; Beth Lundholm, M.S., L.P.; Judy Rand, R.N., N.M.C.C.; John Lardy, M.S.W., L.I.C.S.W.; Billy Anderson, M.A., L.I.C.S.W.; and Megan Baldwin, B.A.

I would like to offer my sincere thanks to Dr. Veronique N. Valliere, Ph.D., for her insight into the chapter on alcohol and abuse, and for her research in this area.

A special thanks to everyone, all of my family, friends and colleagues, who helped me in so many ways.

And most of all, to all of the abusers and victims who can and will change as a result of reading this book.

I pray for an end to relationship violence. I thank and deeply respect all of the people who donate their time as volunteers, victim advocates, therapists and other professionals working to address and end relationship violence.

CHAPTER 1

Defining Violence

David and Sarah have been dating for two months. Her friends have noticed that she spends less time with them, avoids looking anyone in the eye and on occasion has bruises on her arms and face. She quickly explains that she is clumsy "and sometimes David gets a little angry." Her friends express concern about Sarah being abused, but Sarah refuses to listen. That night she and David go out to dinner and she tells him about her conversation with her friends and how they expressed concern about the dating relationship.

David insists that they continue the conversation at his apartment. Without any discussion, he drives her to his home. Inside, David grabs Sarah by the arm, pushes her onto the couch and begins to yell. "You had no business talking to anyone about me! I have never treated you mean!" He proceeds to take his pants off and tells Sarah she had better have sex with him "because you belong to me." David forces Sarah to have sex and in the process he leaves several bruises on her arms, legs and chest. After finishing the act, David tells Sarah that he loves her and that he would never do anything to hurt her.

Examples of abuse such as this one are increasing. Unfortunately, most victims of dating and domestic violence cannot accept the fact that they are victims. Often someone outside the relationship is the first to correctly label the relationship as abusive, long before the victim or the abuser realizes it. This occurs because of the fear, confusion and pain that victims experience. No one likes to admit that he has been a victim of any kind of violence, let alone violence suffered at the hands of someone close and dear. However, with dating violence increasing daily, it is imperative that we educate ourselves about this form of violence.

Our society is relationship orientated. We are social beings by nature. To be happy involves having a partner or a significant other with whom to share our lives. Despite our tendency to socialize and develop relationships with others, however, many of us have not yet learned how to get along with others, nor have we learned how to build and maintain healthy relationships. As we desperately seek to find that special someone to date and eventually marry or make our life partner, we find that we have no guide to tell us when we have found the right person or how to behave toward them.

We place enormous value on education. Today even many menial jobs require a high school diploma. We often spend years at college or graduate school to achieve certain positions; yet we are never directly taught how to fulfill the various roles we play in our personal lives, such as friend, girlfriend or boyfriend, significant other or partner, mother or father, husband or wife. We learn such roles mostly through observing and modeling our behavior after the behavior of others. The problem here is inherent, for those we observe learned by observing others, and so on. Often it is a classic case of the blind leading the blind.

It is little wonder then that we so often hear about child abuse and domestic abuse. We are beginning to accept the fact that violence does occur between married people and to children, but most of us remain ignorant that apart from date rape—which has received attention recently—many other types of abuse occur.

When I lecture in high schools, the students often begin our discussion believing that abuse rarely happens in their dating relationships.

Even as I answer their preliminary questions about what the definitions of abuse are, only a few students label their relationships as abusive. However, after I give examples of the varied types of abuse, over 85 percent of the students state that they have been, are being or know of a friend being abused! It is frightening that between the ages of fifteen and eighteen, most young people have already experienced dating abuse in some way. I have found that the statistics are not much different for adults and college students.

What, then, is abuse?

Abuse refers to any act that is intended to cause or results in harm to another person. Included here are verbal put-downs and name calling on one extreme, to pushing, slapping, rape and murder on the other extreme. The terms *abuse* and *violence* will be used interchangeably throughout this book.

Harm is any emotional, psychological, physical or sexual injury. We may not always be able to see that abuse has occurred. There may be no scars, bruises or bleeding; nevertheless, other factors and symptoms are present.

Victim refers to the person upon whom the violence/abuse is directed. *Abuser* and *perpetrator* refer to the person committing the abuse, and these terms may be used interchangeably. *Significant other, date* and *partner* refer to the person with whom the abuser is involved in a dating relationship.

Intent refers to what a person wants to do—the plan. The concept of intent often causes confusion and it is often believed that abusers do not intend or mean to cause harm. But all abuse is planned. When abuse occurs, it is because of a conscious choice made by the abuser. Abusers make a decision; they give themselves permission to abuse. Intent may be difficult to establish or prove, but if the goal is to create fear, to injure or to gain the cooperation of someone through intimidation, force or injury, then abuse is intentional. Often abusers claim that the abuse was an accident. Accidents do occur, but *abuse toward one's significant other is always a planned choice.* It never occurs by chance.

As to frequency, whether the abusive act occurs only once or several times, it is still abuse.

There are four types of abuse: *emotional, psychological, physical* and *sexual.*

Emotional Abuse

Frank tells Pam that she is not capable of doing anything right. When she does something for him, Frank usually finds something to criticize. Pam finally tells Frank that she is leaving the relationship and Frank says, "Leaving me proves that you always run away when you fail."

Also referred to as verbal abuse, emotional abuse refers to the attacking of someone's self-worth and self-esteem. Emotional abuse makes the victim feel degraded, uneasy, confused and angry. Examples of emotional abuse include name-calling, put-downs, belittling of accomplishments and swearing. This is the most common form of abuse and usually it is present in all other types of abuse. Often people overlook emotional abuse and may accept it as normal behavior. However, it *is* a type of abuse. In most cases the abuser will eventually progress to abusing in other ways and the abuse will become increasingly severe. Emotional abuse marks the beginning of an abusive relationship and should be taken just as seriously as psychological, physical and sexual abuse.

Psychological Abuse

Scott refers to Jean as stupid. He threatens to harm her and then contradicts himself, blaming her for hearing him wrong, in an effort to make Jean appear crazy. When Jean completes her college degree, Scott calls her a "dummy" and belittles her degree as being "easy to get, if you got one." Scott prioritizes everyone and everything before Jean. When Jean ends the relationship, Scott blames her for all of the problems they had.

Psychological abuse refers to the attacking of someone's self-esteem and self-worth, but the attacks are made against the whole being of the other person. Examples include

- threatening to harm the other
- threatening to or actually destroying the other's belongings
- hitting or destroying property (doors, walls, chairs, pictures and so on)
- threatening to or actually taking or harming the children
- monitoring the other's actions (who they talk to, where they go, who they see, and so on)
- withholding and/or controlling the other's money, including taking money and making the other buy things for the abuser
- interrupting eating and/or sleeping patterns
- forcing the other to do anything degrading, humiliating or dangerous
- criticizing the other's thoughts, beliefs or behaviors
- belittling the other's accomplishments
- treating the other as if inferior or a servant

As a result of psychological abuse, the victim may experience fear—of the abuser, of being harmed or of others finding out about the abuse—as well as feelings of being trapped, worthless and exploited.

Psychological abuse involves objectification. This occurs when abusers begin to view their significant others as possessions rather than people. Objectifying their significant others makes it easier for abusers to abuse: it is much easier to harm an object than a person. Name calling and jealousy are part of objectification. The abuser who psychologically abuses his or her significant other will eventually progress to physical and sexual abuse.

Although many people differentiate between emotional and psychological abuse, the differences are small. Both emotional and psychological abuse are attacks upon a person's identity, self-esteem and self-worth; both are abuse. On a scale of severity, these two rank on the bottom, but the effects are often more devastating and long lasting than other forms of abuse.

Physical Abuse

Kathy pinches and slaps Ted when she becomes angry. Ted attempts to calm her down, but his attempts only seem to exacerbate Kathy's rage. Kathy punches him in the eye, which turns black and blue. Ted cannot find a way to tell anyone and he feels trapped.

Reggie is jealous of Samantha. He often feels insecure and blames his feelings on her supposedly seeing other men. Reggie threatens that if she ever cheated on him, he would cut her "so that nobody would ever want you." Reggie slaps Samantha across the face, grabs her by the hair and slams her against the wall.

Physical abuse involves physical attacks, including any unwanted bodily contact. Common examples include

- slapping
- punching
- pushing
- kicking
- grabbing
- choking
- spanking
- wrestling
- pinching
- biting
- scratching
- throwing the other bodily
- burning
- pulling hair
- restraining (holding the other down, not allowing her to leave, etc.)
- using any object or weapon against the other

Emotional and psychological abuse are inherently involved in physical abuse. However, during physical abuse the immediate safety of the victim is in jeopardy. When an abuser has progressed to using physical abuse, she has totally objectified her significant other.

Sexual Abuse

Alex smooth-talks Greta into making out. He promises only to touch her. After several minutes of touching, Alex begins to get rough. He gets on top of Greta, takes off his pants and forces her to have oral sex. He then blames her by saying, "You got me so turned on that I couldn't stop"—which was his plan all along.

Tammy pressures Harry into sexual intercourse. Harry explains that he is tired and not in the mood. He also says that until their relationship deepens, he is not comfortable having intercourse with her. Tammy begins to rub Harry's crotch, pleading with him to have sex with her. She asks him, "What kind of man are you that you don't want to have sex with me? What's wrong with you?" He then complies with her demands out of feelings of guilt, shame and helplessness.

Greg dances with Paul at the bar. As they dance, Greg begins to rub Paul's butt and thighs. Paul removes Greg's hands and tells him to stop. Greg becomes enraged, calls Paul a "bitch," grabs him by the arm and takes him to the back of the bar. Greg tells Paul, "I bought you drinks, I danced with you and you owe me sex. Prove that you care about me." Paul feels obligated to do as Greg says.

Sexual abuse involves attacking someone sexually. This includes any forced sexual contact, whether by coercion (psychological force), physical force, threats or ignoring the other's rights and requests. Examples include

- unwanted sexual comments or gestures
- touching the other sexually without consent

- forcing the other to commit any sexual act against his will, including having sex with others, videotaping, the use of objects and so on
- ignoring the other's *no*s
- intimidating, begging or using love as a means of forcing sexual contact ("Prove that you love me")
- engaging in sexual activity when the other is impaired (sleeping, injured, under the influence of drugs or alcohol) or unable to say no for any reason (does not speak same language, hearing/speech impairment)

Sexual abuse also includes all other types of abuse, because physical contact is made and emotional and psychological abuse are involved. Sexual abuse is *rape*. Sexual abuse is an extremely intricate and complicated topic and for the purpose at hand will be dealt with only as it relates to violence within intimate relationships.

One dating couple I counseled whose relationship had violent aspects was John and Betty. Prior to our session together, John was arrested for physically abusing Betty. When he came in for his initial assessment he greatly minimized his abusive behavior and apologized to Betty if he had hurt her with his yelling and pushing. John made it clear to Betty and me that he never intended to hurt Betty, or anyone for that matter. He stated that if he was under stress and things did not go his way, he could not control his temper. For several sessions John described how he believed he was powerless over his anger and how he was "out of control."

Interestingly, Betty told a different story about John's "powerlessness." She explained that he would be very quiet when something was bothering him and he would distance himself from everyone by keeping a mean and intimidating look on his face. She further described how John would yell at her for anything she did and when she asked him what was wrong, he would become increasingly agitated and angry. Sometimes John would go off by himself, go to his parents' home or hang out with his friends, and when he returned to spend time with Betty he would be calm.

Betty further described how John behaved if he did not leave when he was angry and stressed. He would first appear to pick a fight with her by not leaving her alone and would become more blaming and paranoid as she tried to calm him. At times, he would end up apologizing to her and giving her a hug, after which he would talk about what was bothering him. Other times, however, John became a different man. He threatened to have affairs and also threatened to hurt her. John had slapped Betty, pushed her against the wall and forced her to have sex with him.

When John listened to Betty's description of how he behaved, he first became angry, denying her observations. He blamed her for not listening to him, for being selfish and for not meeting his needs. After some time in therapy, John broke down and cried. I asked him what was wrong and he replied that Betty's assessments were right. He could not believe that he could treat Betty, or anyone for that matter, in such an abusive manner. John's abusive behaviors were traumatic for both of them.

During our sessions John recognized that only he could give himself permission to hurt Betty and that when he gave himself permission to be "out of control" he was actually in total control. John began to realize that by making the decision to abuse Betty, he did intend to cause harm.

Unfortunately, this type of abuse is prevalent. Abuse is pervasive throughout our society and has presented us with a serious chronic problem that, left untreated, will infect the quality of all our relationships.

CHAPTER 2

Forms
of Abuse

Abuse appears in many guises. The easiest way to identify it is by looking for controlling behavior. The purpose of control is to force another person to behave in a specific way. It is almost always abusive. Whether you are the victim or abuser, it is important to identify what type of control has occurred so that it can be directly addressed. Below are some of the most common forms of control that my clients identify. They range from blatant acts to subtle jabs, but all are ways in which abusers attempt to feel more powerful than their victims. Take the time to explore your own relationship to determine what types of control may be occurring.

We can begin by considering what many people think of when they hear the word *abusive*: violent, threatening behavior.

Overt Aggression

Jack slaps Wendy when she refuses to do what he wants. He has even choked her when another male smiled at her.

Phil puts Abe down a lot and has grabbed him by the hair and punched him when angry.

Jack and Phil have something in common—they both use violence when hurt, frustrated or angry.

Overt aggression involves direct, assaultive comments and behaviors. Its primary goal is to instill fear in the partner and gain the upper hand in order to control. Examples include any type of physical abuse or assault, such as punching, slapping and kicking. Overt aggression does not always require direct, physical contact, however: raising a hand as if to hit; driving recklessly, especially with the victim in the car; slamming doors and throwing objects are all acts intended to frighten the victim into submission.

Regardless of the degree of severity, any form of physical abuse is dangerous and will become increasingly severe over time unless the abuser gets into therapy. Physical—and sometimes sexual—abuse differs from other forms of abuse in that it can and does result in serious injury and even death. An extreme example is a nightclub blaze in New York.

An irate abusive man wanted to teach his former girlfriend a lesson. He set fire to the nightclub she visited. The result was that more than eighty people were killed and many others were seriously injured.

There is never justification for the stupidity of violence and in the end many innocent people may be affected.

Explosive behavior sends a loud and clear message that a person is dangerous and will not consider the safety of his partner when he becomes angry. Individuals with explosive behavior need specialized psychological intervention including anger management treatment.

Intimidation, Threats and Subtle Aggression

Peter often tells Marsha's friends that she is unfaithful to him and he tells everyone that they are having sex when in fact Marsha has refused to be sexual with him. Peter occasionally yells at her and physically blocks the door to prevent Marsha from leaving. As a result, Marsha often complies with his demands for forced sexual contact and is subsequently raped.

Susan wants Henry to give her fine jewelry and has told him to buy the gifts for her or she will have an affair. Susan states that if Henry refuses, she may tell his parents that he abuses her.

Intimidation is the act of reminding the victim of the abuser's power and how it could be used against the victim. Methods vary by abuser. In some cases, a look or stare may signal danger to a victim; in others, the abuser may yell or hold an object as though preparing to throw it at the victim. Subtle aggression involves behavior that implies the possibility of escalation or that has led to overt aggression in the past. Examples include gunning the accelerator of the car or talking in a menacing or condescending tone of voice. Some abusers may talk about past abusive episodes.

Threats are a direct verbal or nonverbal statement that if one fails to do as told, consequences and harm will occur. They are closely related to intimidation and at times it is impossible to tell the difference. Threats include giving verbal or physical warning to the victim of impending harm—that is, letting the victim know that the abuser will harm him if he does not do as the abuser says. The harm may be directed toward the victim or others and may include threats to damage or destroy property or to injure children or pets. Often threats include spreading vicious rumors or even telling others personal truths that may emotionally harm the victim.

Some abusers threaten to commit suicide, or, in extreme cases, to murder their victims. Although threats of either suicide or homicide need to be taken seriously, in most cases the abuser cares about himself far too much to harm himself and most often needs his partner to continue in the role of victim far too much to fatally wound her. If the abuser chooses suicide, it is his own choice and only qualified mental health professionals may help such a person. The best thing to do with someone who threatens suicide is to encourage that person to seek counseling. The responsibility of choosing suicide rests with the person threatening to harm himself. No one else is ever to blame for a suicide's morbid choice of acts.

Because it is difficult to identify which abusers will follow through with their threats, if an abuser threatens a person's life, the threats should be taken very seriously. Police protection must be sought. An abuser who threatens to kill has progressed to the end of the violence continuum and is not likely to change. Professional intervention is warranted.

Intimidation and threats are clearly controlling and abusive behaviors. They cause the victim to have to protect himself and are often attempts to force the victim to back down and give in to the abuser's demands. Making insinuations that harm may occur is not a loving act.

Boundary Violations

Elaine makes comments about Jessie's body when he is within hearing range. She tells him, "I think you have a sexy body and would love to touch you all over." Jessie feels uncomfortable with Elaine's comments and tells her to stop, that he does not want to be talked to like a sex object.

Victor makes sexual gestures towards Renee when they are alone. He grabs his crotch, blows kisses and moves close to her, sometimes rubbing against her. She has told him to stop and that she is not interested in him. He ignores her requests.

Everyone has beliefs about what treatment is acceptable. This may include concepts of personal space, what type of touching is permissible under what circumstances and what language should be used towards other people. Overstepping such limits when another person has made them clear is a violation of personal boundaries. Engaging in any behavior towards a person without his or her permission is a deliberate act of disrespect. It minimizes the feelings and value of the victim.

Harassment

Harassment is any behavior that causes fear, intimidation or nuisance to another person. This includes continuing to engage in some type of behavior or contact that you have been told to stop or that you are aware is unwanted by another person. It is important to understand that if a reasonable person would be aware that the contact or behavior is unwanted or inappropriate, then the abuser cannot justify his actions by claiming that he was not aware that they were unwanted. Using offensive language or gestures, making demeaning jokes or repeatedly telephoning someone who has indicated that the calls are unwelcome are all ways to demonstrate control. They are the abuser's way of stating that he or she can choose to treat the victim as unimportant.

Stalking

In an article published in the *American Journal of Criminal Law*, C. Perez defines stalking as "willful, malicious, and repeated following and harassing of another person that threatens his or her safety." Stalking is not an act of love or devotion but a threat evidenced by the intrusion in the victim's life. It is a way of venting anger or hostility towards the victim. The stalker seeks to exert power and control and to cause the victim fear.

Stalkers show up in places where their presence is unwelcome or not allowed, including victims' homes, workplaces and recreational activities. Any unwelcome communication can be a form of stalking. This includes making unwanted telephone calls, sending letters, packages or emails, or using other people to convey messages.

Rather than following the victim, some stalkers focus on gathering personal information. They may surveil victims' homes or have other people tail victims. Monitoring or recording another person's telephone conversation is a form of stalking, as is reading or interfering with any of the other person's communications such as mail or messages.

In more extreme cases, stalking may involve breaking and entering. Sometimes property is damaged; some stalkers may injure or kill victims' pets. They may leave things or rearrange victims' belongings. Stalkers can be dangerous and may physically assault or even kidnap their victims.

Violating Agreements or Court Orders

In recognition of the threat abusers pose to their victims, the courts may issue orders limiting contact. Unfortunately, abusers do not always obey them. Violation of a no contact order, a restraining order, an order for protection or any other official agreement of restricted contact is almost always intentional and rarely a mistake or misunderstanding. In fact, the court makes sure that the other person understands the limitations. Yet abusers are very good at finding exceptions to the rule and inventing loopholes. Any violation of a court order should be taken very seriously and reported to the authorities.

Obeying court orders limiting or preventing contact is the responsibility of the person being restricted, not of the victim. This means that even if the victim invites the abuser to get together, the abuser can still be imprisoned for violating the order. If the abuser shows up at the same restaurant as the victim, it is the abuser's responsibility to leave immediately, even if he arrived first. There is no exception to the order unless the court grants special permission in advance.

Also remember that passing messages, even through third parties such as mutual friends or the children, is restricted. If a no contact order has been issued, the abuser should not communicate with the victim.

The fact that relationships are subject to laws brings up an important point: no relationship exists in a vacuum. You and your partner live in a real world and are surrounded by other people. Abusers often take advantage of this fact and use others to aid in their control of victims.

Using the Children

Floyd has been separated from his wife Donna for two months. When Floyd spends time with their children, he often questions them about their mother and puts her down in front of them. When Donna confronts him about his conduct, he threatens to withhold child support payments and even to cancel special events he had planned with the children.

Using children occurs when one or both persons in a relationship are parents and one manipulates the children to create fear or guilt in order to gain the cooperation of the other. This is common when separation or divorce occurs. In some cases, the abuser directly threatens to harm the children if the victim does not behave in a certain way, but some abusers use the children more subtly. Often the abuser involves the children in things that should not be the concern of children. One parent may engage in behavior I refer to as "adultifying" or "parentifying" the child, giving the child adult power to make decisions that children typically do not make for themselves. Common examples of this include allowing the children to set their own curfews, involving the children in discussions about household finances and discussing marital concerns with the children.

Abusers may also attempt to pit the children against the other parent. Some may give the children special gifts. By refusing to punish or failing to support the other parent's disciplinary action, the abuser can make the victim appear to be the mean parent and undermine the children's respect for the victim. An abuser may also make promises to the children on the victim's behalf without first ensuring that the victim can fulfill them: the abuser may tell the children the other parent will spend time with them on a certain day, for instance, without making sure that the other parent is free that day.

Another strategy abusers may use to win the favor of the children away from the victim is what I refer to as "incestuosity"—that is, befriending a child as if he or she were an adult and involving intimate or romantic behavior, regardless of whether the behavior reaches direct sexual contact. The child may not recognize the inappropriate nature of this interaction and may only feel that one parent treats him or her specially. Examples of this include

- using intimate physical behavior more frequently than prior to the marital problems becoming significant (e.g., hugging more often; sitting closer to the child; kissing more frequently, especially on the lips)
- buying or allowing the child to wear sexy lingerie or skimpy clothing
- telling the children intimate and personal information about either parent

When a couple has had a child together but one person attempts to terminate the relationship, an abuser may use the child to try to trap the victim into remaining in the relationship. This occurs when the abuser threatens to get custody of the child (without regard for the child's well-being), requests unreasonable visitations with the child or refuses to make child support payments. An abuser may even attempt to make the other parent appear unfit to have custody of the child. This creates fear in the victim and he may choose to remain in the relationship for fear of losing the child. This is abuse.

Using children as pawns of revenge to cause discomfort in anyone is not only abusive but repulsive. Any time children are used in this fashion, the abuser's visitation with the children should be ceased.

Economic Abuse

Jan expects Paul to spend much of his money on her and sometimes gets angry when he does not spend as much as she wants. She punishes him by refusing dates and sex when he does not do as she demands.

Rick demands that Angie pay for his fun and often uses her charge cards and expects that she should pay. When she tells him that she cannot afford to pay his bills, he becomes angry and blackmails her into paying by threatening to end the relationship, taking with him all the things that he charged on her credit cards.

Misspending money is controlling because most people are on budgets. Extravagant spending or failure to pay financial obligations may place a partner in dire straits. The threat of having a negative credit history, accumulating significant financial debt or not having enough money to pay the necessary bills can be very overwhelming. Placing such a burden on a partner is abusive. When partners share a budget, especially when one has given up work to raise the children, money can be a weapon.

Once thought to occur only in marriages, economic abuse is also very common in dating relationships. It results in the victim losing a sense of control, happiness and responsibility that making money can bring.

Depending on the relationship, a couple might or might not choose to share financial information and resources. Either arrangement can work as long as both partners agree and are held to equal conditions. One partner should not expect the other to report all income but refuse to do the same. If both partners are living together and have steady incomes, it is inappropriate for one to expect the other to pay for all household expenses. If a couple has chosen to share their incomes, withholding or hiding money is unethical. One partner should not open bank accounts without informing the other—although, of course, this is not abusive or controlling when the victim of abuse is secretly establishing financial security to utilize if he or she must leave in a hurry. Making one's significant other pay for one's bills or making the victim ask for her own money is wrong. Adults do not receive an allowance and have the right to refuse to spend money on their significant others without needing an excuse.

Isolation

Carol and Beth have been dating for several months. Carol becomes jealous of Beth's friends. She demands that Beth run all plans through Carol and get permission. Carol has even sabotaged Beth's plans and expects that Beth will spend all of her time with her.

A major part of controlling someone is controlling how he spends his time and with whom. This may involve sabotaging friendships, indirectly or directly attempting to discourage others from wanting to be around the victim or telling a partner straight out that she cannot spend time with certain people.

Isolation often occurs in abusive relationships and can be an important force preventing a victim from seeking help and assistance. When an abuser keeps the victim from seeing another person, the abuser effectively prevents the victim from gaining the support necessary to aid in leaving the abuser or ending the relationship. If the abuser keeps the victim from attending school or work, the victim may lose self-esteem, as well as the sense of accomplishment that comes from attaining goals. The abuser may actually feel threatened if the victim attains a college or graduate degree, believing that the victim may become more intelligent and knowledgeable than the abuser and may be better able to leave the relationship and survive.

Abusers use many strategies to limit their victims' support networks. Common examples include

- withholding messages or mail from others
- telling people not to contact the victim or that they cannot see her
- telling callers that the victim does not want to talk with them when in fact he does
- telling people a partner is not at home to take a call when in fact she is
- behaving towards the victim's support network in such a manner that others choose to avoid the couple
- prohibiting a victim from spending time with others without the abuser (This causes even more difficulty when combined with the preceding example.)
- telling people lies about a partner to discourage continued contact

If you know someone who has been cut off in this way, it is possible that he or she is being abused and needs help.

Isolation scars. At times it can lead to lasting emotional damage, because it encourages the victim to feeling helpless, alone and trapped. Being isolated also increases the chance of the victim believing that abuse is a natural, accepted form of expression, because there may not be access to healthy relationships with which to compare the current relationship. Isolation may also increase the victim's belief that the abuse is her own fault, that somehow the abuse is deserved (which is *never* the case).

Treating Others Respectfully, but Not One's Partner

This strategy to keep a partner under the abuser's control and doubting his own sanity occurs commonly. In addition to making others believe that she is a nice, nonabusive person, the abuser seeks to increase the painful impact of her mistreatment of the victim. When she treats everyone but her partner with respect, her partner may experience lowered self-esteem and a diminished sense of self-worth. This may also further isolate the victim from supportive relationships by causing others to view the victim as the problem, perhaps believing that he is overreacting.

For these reasons, abusers may behave politely and respectfully in the company of others, only to become abusive when alone with a partner. The abuser may purposely engage in conversation or contact with others with the intention of portraying a calm and respectful demeanor. An abuser may even go so far as to claim the victim's support network for himself, establishing contact with the network before the victim can in an attempt to give his side of the story first.

Making a Partner Appear Crazy

People outside of a relationship often trust one partner to accurately represent the other. This puts an abuser in a position to lie about the victim and lead others to conclude that the victim is irresponsible, mentally unstable or in need of some type of professional help. Such behavior often goes hand-in-hand with manipulation. Common examples include

- changing plans at the last minute and telling others that the victim had been informed of the change long ago

- making plans and telling others that the victim will participate, but failing to inform the victim
- quietly beginning a fight or argument while around others so
  that when the victim responds, it appears that the victim began
  the argument

When a victim's support network and family begin to side with
her spouse, believing whatever he says, the victim loses vital support.
The abuser then uses this against the victim. The results are increased
isolation and new ammunition.

Abusers also tend to calm down quickly after an argument or
abuse, leaving the victim agitated and shaken. To others, the victim
appears to be unstable. When the police arrive at the scene of a
domestic assault, quite often the abuser has deescalated and appears
calm, because he has vented his anger; the victim, on the other hand,
is understandably unable just to let go and calm down. As a result, the
abuser appears to be the credible one and, in some cases, convinces the
police that he is in fact the victim.

Portraying the Victim as the Abuser

Abusers often complain to others to portray themselves as victims.
This can be done behind the true victim's back or in full view. By presenting his version of the problems first, the abuser attempts to make
the victim's version appear to be an excuse or retaliation. The victim
may seem guilty or defensive if he tells the truth after others have heard
the abuser. This becomes controlling because it limits the availability of
support for the victim. In addition, the victim may be forced to explain
to others why his significant other would be complaining or making
allegations, perhaps making the victim appear vindictive.

Jealousy

Jealousy involves protecting objects and belongings from being
taken away. People are not objects. We cannot be owned or stolen.
Being jealous is a form of objectification. If a person's partner decides
to have an affair or to terminate the relationship, she will do so, not

because someone stole her, but because she made the conscious decision to do so.

If others are staring at or flirting with your significant other, that is nothing to worry about. If your significant other is flirting back, then it is an issue to be discussed. If he or she continues to flirt after you have expressed your concerns and dislike for that behavior, that may be an indication that he or she is not happy in the relationship. Perhaps couples therapy is necessary; perhaps the relationship is finished. In any case, recognize that your significant other is the only person in control of his or her behavior.

Remember that when others are flirting with your partner, that is a compliment. Would you really want to be married to someone who was not attractive to others? Also remember that those who are validating the beauty of your spouse are only getting to glance; your spouse is going home with you, not them!

Jealousy is generally the result of insecurity and frustration. Demonstrating it is abusive and controlling and reveals a lack of respect. For a more thorough analysis of jealousy, look at Chapter 8 of this book.

Openly discussing one's discomfort with a partner's flirtatious behavior towards others can be an important step towards resolving a problem. This is only one example of the vital role communication plays in any healthy relationship. Unfortunately, it can also be distorted and used as a form of control.

Ordering and Pressuring

Sara pressures Mike to take her to an upcoming concert instead of his awards ceremony. She continues to beg, saying, "Oh, come on …please." Mike feels the pressure from Sara and feels he needs to take care of Sara's demands.

Ordering involves demanding that a partner do things rather than making requests or politely asking. Pressuring means repeatedly reminding a partner of something, such as one's expectations and wants, without regard for his emotional or physical well being. It entails begging, pleading and nagging until a victim cannot refuse without feeling guilty, selfish or abnormal. This is controlling and abusive not only because of its impact on a partner's behavior, but also because it implies that the victim and her desires are less important than the abuser's. The abuser orders because he believes that he has the power to do so and that the victim lacks the power to refuse.

Demanding to Talk or to Resolve a Problem

Demanding to talk or to solve a problem is abusive and controlling when one partner relentlessly pesters the other into a conversation that the latter has already said he is not comfortable having. It is fair to say that there are issues that are so serious that we may attempt to force others to address them. However, if a person refuses to discuss the issues, then her partner does not have the right to continue to badger him or her. Attempts to force someone to talk include

- following a partner around the house
- not allowing the partner to fall asleep
- repeatedly calling
- physically abusing a partner to get him or her to listen and talk
- continuing to discuss the problem even after reaching an apparent solution or compromise or impasse

Refusing to Talk

Silence is a remarkably effective form of abuse. Without ongoing, direct communication, the relationship is doomed to fail. It is nearly impossible for two people to meet each other's needs when one is not expressing hers. Common examples include

- refusing to state what one wants or needs
- telling the victim that something is wrong, but failing to say what
- giving the silent treatment
- sulking

To say that refusing to talk and demanding to talk are both abusive behaviors may seem almost contradictory. How can one possibly communicate? This question is answered more thoroughly in Chapter 14; however, the main point to remember now is that communication should be a respectful process between equals and not a demonstration of one partner's power over the other.

Ignoring

Refusing to listen to someone, failing to respond to his or her needs or requests and looking right over him or her are all ways of discounting the worth of another person. Like demanding or refusing to talk, ignoring also damages communication, harming the relationship. Common examples include

- refusing to acknowledge a partner's presence or wishes
- pretending to be listening without actually paying attention
- forcing a partner to repeat himself by not listening.
- turning up the volume of the radio or television when the victim is on the phone or talking with someone

Lying or Withholding Information

Cindy promised Nathan when he took her to a concert that they would go steady. The day after the concert, she told him, "Thanks, it was fun, but I only wanted to go to the concert."

Deceit is an obvious form of control. By distorting the truth and withholding information, the abuser attempts to control her partner's reaction and to avoid the consequences of information becoming known.

An abuser may claim that he did not actually lie when, for instance, he shared only the verifiable details and withheld or even blatantly denied other facts that were less likely to be exposed. She may tell the truth only when it is too late for the victim to act on the information; for example, the abuser may hide invitations from the victim's social support network until after the event has occurred. Any way in which one partner deliberately causes another to construct false beliefs is lying. The exact method does not matter: withholding information, distorting facts and admitting the truth only when confronted are all forms of abuse.

Lying occurs when the abuser makes a conscious decision to mislead the other person. It is not an accident or a situation where the abuser "just forgot" or "just did not think it was important." The human brain is an amazing organ. It does not forget as often as many people would like to believe it does. The mind remembers even the smallest, most insignificant detail of an event or situation. Whether we choose to call a memory to mind is really the question. In my many years of experience, I have found that abusers can almost always recall every detail of something that happened when pressured to do so. Only those with true brain injury or those with severe, chronic alcohol or drug problems can justifiably use forgetting as an excuse for withholding information.

Criticizing and Discounting

Criticizing means the repeated putting down of a partner's beliefs, behavior, abilities or worth as a human being. Discounting involves belittling a partner's accomplishments, skill and opinions. These are ways for one partner to attempt to take a superior stance over the other. Common examples include

- calling attention to a partner's failings in unconstructive ways
- putting a partner down for his statements or behavior in private or in public
- telling a partner that she does not know what she is talking about
- making comments such as, "Like that really matters," "So what?" and "But can you answer this…"
- bringing up an irrelevant topic solely to demonstrate a partner's lack of knowledge about that subject

Name Calling

Name calling demonstrates a person's willingness to objectify and put down a partner when angry, rather than attempting to discuss the problem in a respectful manner. Victims of name-calling tend to doubt their self-worth and may begin to blame themselves for the problem.

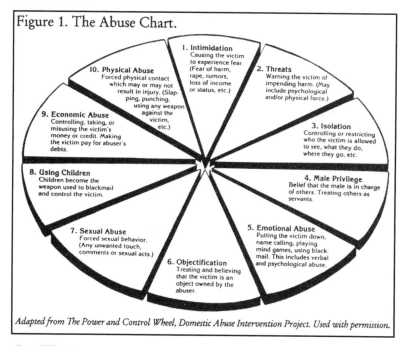

Figure 1. The Abuse Chart.

1. Intimidation
Causing the victim to experience fear. (Fear of harm, rape, rumors, loss of income or status, etc.)

2. Threats
Warning the victim of impending harm. (May include psychological and/or physical force.)

3. Isolation
Controlling or restricting who the victim is allowed to see, what they do, where they go, etc.

4. Male Privilege
Belief that the male is in charge of others. Treating others as servants.

5. Emotional Abuse
Putting the victim down, name calling, playing mind games, using blackmail. This includes verbal and psychological abuse.

6. Objectification
Treating and believing that the victim is an object owned by the abuser.

7. Sexual Abuse
Forced sexual behavior. (Any unwanted touch, comments or sexual acts.)

8. Using Children
Children become the weapon used to blackmail and control the victim.

9. Economic Abuse
Controlling, taking, or misusing the victim's money or credit. Making the victim pay for abuser's debts.

10. Physical Abuse
Forced physical contact which may or may not result in injury. (Slapping, punching, using any weapon against the victim, etc.)

Adapted from The Power and Control Wheel, Domestic Abuse Intervention Project. Used with permission.

Sarcasm

Sarcasm generally involves the use of slanted, indirect comments to express anger or discontent. Some abusers make demeaning remarks about victims and claim afterwards they were "only kidding" to avoid the consequences. Biting humor may be used to convey a message. Many people use sarcasm to joke, but even jokes may be interpreted as insults, intentional or not. If one partner is the butt of every joke, power may not be evenly shared. When sarcasm becomes a hurtful pattern of interaction or language, it becomes abusive.

Apologizing

Apologizing is usually a healthy and respectful thing to do. However, it becomes abusive and controlling when apologies come too quickly, either without an understanding of what was said or done that was offensive or without any intention to avoid the same behavior in the future. Apologies can be sarcastic; an abuser may say "I'm sorry" in a tone that belittles the victim and his distress.

Abusers often apologize and expect victims simply to accept the apology and move on. However, to assume that a victim is able or willing to forgive and forget abusive comments or behavior is unrealistic and disrespectful. First, the human mind cannot selectively erase memories. Second, a victim should not forget what occurred even if it were possible, because change must happen. When abuse and control are ongoing, apologies are worse than meaningless: they are the abuser's way of keeping the victim from escaping the relationship.

Sarcastic and insincere apologies are effective ways for an abuser to manipulate his victim's emotions. The abuser invents a scenario where he is put-upon or mistreated by being forced to apologize. There are several other ways in which an abuser may try to pass off a distorted account as reality in an attempt to gain power over a victim.

Blaming

Abusers refuse to accept any responsibility for relationship problems and so blame the victims. They fail to acknowledge their own roles or accept very minor or insignificant pieces. Even events that are clearly beyond the victim's control may be attributed to the victim; for instance, an abuser may claim that a speeding ticket was the direct result of how upset she was because of something the victim said or did. Some abusers accuse their victims of holding them back from better jobs. By refusing to accept responsibility for his actions, the abuser denies his ability to change. In addition, he places a burden of guilt on the victim.

Emotional Blackmail

Gene tells Gail, "If you love me, prove it. I've been dating you so long, you owe me sex. I've spent so much money on you, you're indebted to me." Gail experiences guilt, powerlessness and a sense of obligation.

Emotional blackmail refers to using emotions or personal information to pressure or force another person into compliance. Its goal is to equate feelings of care and love with obedience. Abusers commonly use guilt, shame or fear of abandonment to manipulate victims. They may take advantage of a partner's emotional state or prior emotional problems to coerce compliance. The victim becomes confused, begins to question whether she is giving enough to the abuser or relationship and experiences a sense of obligation to do what the abuser demands.

These strategies are often used to pressure a partner into sexual contact she does not want. Sex is never something that is owed, but rather is a shared privilege. Statements such as "If you love me, prove it," "If you loved me, you would do what I am telling you" and "I've been dating you for so long and have spent so much money on you that you now owe me sex" are examples of emotional blackmail.

Neglect and Abandonment

Refusing to assume any responsibility for the relationship indicates a lack of emotional investment. Neglect is controlling because it compels one partner to take drastic action to get the other reinvested. It forces one person to take on more responsibilities than an individual could be expected to handle. Consider what each of the following examples indicates about the abuser's view of the victim and the relationship:

- allowing or demanding that the other person take charge of the relationship or any major decisions
- spending more time with others or working too many hours to avoid spending time with the victim
- establishing new routines or activities that require more time out of the home
- failing to fulfill obligations to the victim

Such behavior sends the message that the relationship and the victim are unimportant to the abuser and unworthy of his or her attention.

Competition

Healthy relationships require a large degree of equality in most areas of the relationship. When one person becomes overly competitive, it becomes impossible to share intimacy. A victim can hardly relax or feel secure in a relationship if he is constantly being judged. This prevents the relationship from growing in a healthy direction. A partner who always has to be right takes a toll on a person, making him feel less competent than that partner.

Some abusers create competition in every area of life. They cannot be the last to finish getting dressed in the morning. An afternoon stroll turns into a fast-paced speed walk. Others take conventional forms of competition to unhealthy extremes: they may not be able to stand losing a board game or a game of pool. To such people, achievement only counts if it is perfect and anything less than first place is unacceptable.

Playing Mind Games

Mind games are a form of manipulation in which the abuser tricks the victim into giving in to demands. The abuser deliberately misreads situations, intentions or comments. Common examples include

- doing the opposite of what was asked
- repeatedly making the same comments or requests and making it appear that she has not made those comments or requests before
- setting a partner up to get mad and then taking a victim stance when it happens

Such behaviors are often confusing and disorienting to the victim, who may give in to the abuser's requests in an effort to restore some sanity to life.

Playing Psychologist

Sometimes an abuser assumes a helper role or analyzes what the victim says and does. This changes the balance of power in the relationship from fairly equal to a one-up/one-down situation.

Of course, crises can occur and there are times when one person may need psychological support from the other. But these occasions should remain few and far between and occur only if both agree to the temporary shift in power. If two people first meet at a time when one is in crisis and the other in a helping or supportive role, it is unlikely that a healthy relationship will ever be established. Healthy relationships require that both people have equal power and that both are emotionally stable.

Inequality

Inequality is the heart of abuse. It means just what it sounds like: an unequal value is given to one person in the relationship. This often has to do with resentments or narcissism. The abuser believes that he or she is somehow better, more competent and more important than his or her partner. Behaviors that may indicate inequality in a relationship include attempting to make most decisions for one's partner or belittling the decisions she does make, attempting to take charge of all activities or demonstrating an arrogant and superior attitude.

As you may have noticed, many of the abuse categories share common characteristics with other categories. The lines that separate one form of control from another are often difficult to see. It is not important to make such distinctions. I have found in my work with clients that when people have become abusive, they engage in many of the types of control.

One couple I counseled, Sheryl and Greg, had been dating for several months. They came to me at the request of a college counseling center to deal with what appeared to be abusive tendencies in the way they treated each other. They had hopes of marrying each other and were disturbed at how often they argued. It was determined that there had not been any threat of or actual physical abuse.

Greg admitted to being overly demanding of Sheryl's time. "I become jealous when other men show an interest in her," he said.

Sheryl pointed out, "He makes it a point to make sure that whatever man I am talking with knows we are a couple. Greg comes up to them, puts his arm around me and passionately kisses me." He would then introduce himself as Sheryl's boyfriend and not leave them alone. Sheryl would become annoyed and eventually angry that Greg did not trust her. She would then refuse to have sex with Greg. Greg responded by calling her a tease and accusing her of having sex with other men.

What became painfully obvious was that their relationship lacked trust and both had serious unresolved issues that had not been identified or explored. Greg recalled being physically abused by his father and that his mother would often justify the abuse by blaming it on Greg's lack of commitment to the family. His parents rarely spent time with him and when they did they usually broke any promises made to him. Sheryl's family was not physically abusive, but it lacked emotional intimacy. Her parents constantly criticized her and were never satisfied with her accomplishments, despite the fact that she was a straight-A student heading for a good career.

Because of their childhoods, Greg and Sheryl both learned a traumatic lesson: when they trusted the people they were supposed to (their parents), they were let down. As a result, neither could become emotionally intimate with anyone without expecting to be let down. When they were not let down, both sabotaged the relationship to justify arguing, which served the purpose of preventing them from developing an emotionally deeper relationship. Neither was able to open up to the other about his or her problems and neither could risk being vulnerable to the other.

Their communication was usually superficial. Each wanted to love the other, but both lacked the skills to let their guard down long enough to risk trusting. Just as their parents had used several forms of abuse on them, they in turn began to abuse each other. Greg's abuse of Sheryl took the forms of objectifying, emotional abuse, jealousy and the use of male privilege. Sheryl's abuse of Greg took the form of emotional and sexual abuse (by withholding sex as punishment).

Abusive behavior is used for achieving power and control over another person. I am not implying that power and control are always bad, because we cannot survive without a sufficient amount of both in our lives. However, when the end result or purpose is to abuse, hurt or not respect someone, then such behavior is unhealthy and wrong. If you are being abused, your significant other is telling you loudly and clearly, *"I do not love you!"*

CHAPTER 3

The Abuse Cycle

Violence within any relationship, especially a dating relationship, is a complex pattern of behaviors. The *abuse cycle* adapted from Lenore Walker illustrates this pattern by defining three stages that make up the abuse cycle: *escalation, explosion* and *honeymoon* (see Figure 2).

Although this cycle does help to point out a progression of thoughts, behaviors and emotions, I believe we can go a step deeper and break down these three stages to understand how the decision to act out violently occurs. Let us therefore view the cycle of abuse as fourteen stages clustered into three groups. What was called the escalation stage actually consists of stages one through six of the new model. Stages seven through nine make up what was the explosion stage. The honeymoon stage now consists of stages ten through fourteen. Each stage can be identified by a specific collection of behaviors, emotions and thoughts. The most common forms of these are listed here in tables.

Each individual expresses each leg of the cycle in unique ways. If you ever behave abusively, recognizing the cognitions and behaviors you associate with each phase is a valuable exercise. As you read about the common expressions of each stage, ask yourself what you do, feel and think at that point in your personal cycle. Create your own tables

Figure 2

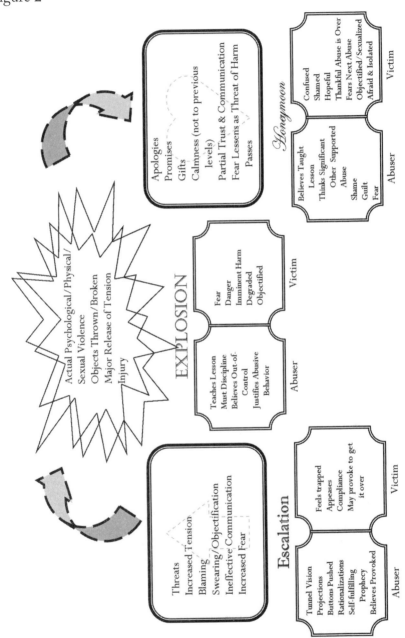

When Sam talks with Karen, she becomes irritable and focuses only on a single point. Karen raises her voice, crosses her arms and makes intense eye contact with Sam. Sam cannot understand what is happening. When he asks her to stop yelling for a moment, Karen becomes defensive and storms out of the room. Sam noticed that Karen was escalating and attempted to settle the situation down to calmly discuss the problem at hand.

People go through a buildup of tension called the escalation stages before they act abusively. A complex pattern of emotions, thoughts, beliefs and decisions occurs prior to action taking place. Some abusers may also begin verbally or psychologically abusing during these stages. The escalation stages are the most important to understand, because recognizing when the cycle is beginning offers an early opportunity to leave the situation or take a time-out.

Six types of cues indicate impending abuse. *Physical signs*; *red flag words, phrases and situations*; and *fantasies* tend to remain consistent, so my explanations of them are generalized across the six stages of escalation. Like the other stages, each escalation stage also has characteristic *behaviors, emotions* and *thoughts and self-talk*, which vary as the abuser moves through the individual stages; these will be presented both in overview and in tables for each stage.

Physical

Physically the abuser's body begins to show signs of increased arousal, also known as the state of fight or flight response. Common examples include making a fist, increased heart rate, squinting the eyes, heavy breathing, tensing jaw muscles and puffing out the chest. Some people experience headaches, stomachaches, acid reflux and muscle tightness and spasms.

Pay attention to your body as you escalate. Ask yourself how it feels and what is it doing. Watch yourself in a mirror when escalating. Document your observations as part of your list of cues.

modeled on the ones in this chapter. Write down the behavic
tions and self-talk that you go through during each stage.

Victims can often complete these tables for their abusers
been on the reciprocal end, they may have noticed things to w
perpetrator would not have been paying close attention. WI
abuser and victim are willing to participate in therapy, I often
independently to write out each stage of the cycle for the mo
abusive episode. Both the victim and the abuser describe the
experiences for this exercise. What is amazing is that with t
ing participants, the cycles often come out to be extremely si
each other. The abuser often gains significant insight from
tim's perceptions.

When beginning to record your own cycle, it is often he
focus on the most recent or most severe abusive incident t
occurred. However, throughout treatment, I strongly encour
to add to the cycle any and all behaviors, emotions and self-t
occur during any abusive incidents. In this way you will b
develop your own encyclopedia of how you act, think and fee
you are at this stage.

Understanding the abuse cycle allows us to recognize, prev
treat abuse. The more aware of his or her cycle an abuser is, th
opportunities he or she has to recognize the cycle and to
healthy, adaptive coping techniques and strategies to successfu
minate the cycle. No one is ever powerless to end the cycle. I
one must invest significant energy to remain in it.

The Escalation Stages

*Doug gets home from work and tells Heidi that she'd better l
him alone. He paces the room, grabs a beer and yells at Heidi to
him something to eat. Heidi asks what is wrong and tries to give
a hug. Doug begins to think in distorted ways and blames her fo
bad day. Heidi recognizes Doug's escalation and chooses to leave
alone, realizing that he will not hear anything she has to say. She
seen him act this way before.*

Red Flag Words, Phrases and Situations

Often abusers speak of "buttons" being pushed. I refer to this as the "He/She made me do it" syndrome. Society reinforces this concept of people having buttons that directly cause us to behave in certain manners. It is often thought that violence occurs in response to certain situations or events. The reality, however, is that abuse does not just happen. No one actually loses control; rather, a conscious choice or decision is made to project responsibility onto one's significant other, that is, to blame the victim.

"Buttons" refer to key words, statements or situations to which we typically respond. For example, when a significant other disappoints an abuser by canceling a date, the abuser may respond by experiencing hurt or disappointment, which he may then quickly turn into anger. What the abuser would remember about this situation is that the canceled date resulted in anger, conveniently forgetting about the hurt he experienced or the excuse given for breaking the date. Certain words and phrases can also act as emotionally charged put-downs. Examples include names that highlight emotional sore spots, such as vulgar names, ethnic slurs and nicknames that a person particularly dislikes. Abusers tend to overreact to red flag words and phrases and often will use them to justify the decision to begin the escalation stage.

Reality disproves the "button" excuse, because if an abuser were truly controlled by buttons, then he or she would respond the same way each and every time the same situation occurred and toward whoever "pushed" the "button," not just toward a significant other.

Even though words and situations do not cause abuse, it is valuable to recognize those that tend to precede it. Like other cues, they are a way to identify the escalation stage and offer an opportunity to choose a healthier response.

Fantasies

Fantasies are thoughts about something that has not yet happened. Common healthy fantasies include thinking about a vacation one will take, imagining a new car or home or simply daydreaming about going out on a date or out on the town for an evening. Fantasies help people plan for the future and everyone has them, but they can become unhealthy in several ways.

When fantasies become expectations, they may lead to frustration. For instance, imagining that one's partner will want to be sexual at a given time does not guarantee that this will happen; however, in the mind of an abuser, it should. The abuser who expected an enthusiastic lover and finds a tired partner who just wants to cuddle may feel as though he is being denied something that had been promised, although of course this is not true.

It is also common for abusers to fantasize about and prepare for what victims may say or do—that is, to role-play situations in their own minds even before the confrontation occurs. This allows the abuser to plan and be aware of her future actions, creating a self-fulfilling prophecy. A self-fulfilling prophecy occurs when one has a thought or plan and acts in ways to make it come true. The story of Gene and Allen illustrates how this happens.

> *Gene thinks that Allen will probably start arguing and complaining as soon as Gene walks in the door after work. By the time he gets home, Gene is already so frustrated with Allen that he goes straight inside without bothering to take off his muddy boots even though he knows that bothers Allen. As Gene expected, Allen complains about the mess on the floor.*

Are there things you often imagine immediately before you begin to escalate? Do you find certain fantasies in your mind at the same time as the other escalation cues are occurring? Add these to your list.

Behaviors

These are the things an abuser does as he or she escalates. Common examples include pacing, shouting, raising one's fist or leg as if to hit or kick, becoming argumentative, drinking or drug use, staring the victim down and physically cornering the victim.

To determine your behavioral cues, ask yourself how you behave when escalating or becoming angry. What actions are parts of a pattern?

Emotions

Abusers experience many emotions, but during these stages most emotions are labeled together as anger. This occurs as a result of not knowing how to identify and express emotions appropriately. For example, many people struggle with feelings of disappointment, abandonment, shame, frustration, hurt or embarrassment. It often seems easier and safer to become depressed or angry rather than accept the vulnerability of experiencing complex emotions, but this only pushes away people who could offer needed support.

Because recognizing the true emotion can be tricky, many people struggle when it comes to listing their emotional escalation cues. If anger is the only cue you come up with for this category of your list, try a slightly different approach: identify the emotions that you experience the most difficulty expressing.

Thoughts and Self-Talk

Thoughts and self-talk refer to the beliefs we hold and the process by which we evaluate the events or situations we experience. Basically we decide how to respond to an event or situation and what it means. Then we use our evaluation of the events to decide which emotion and behavior seems appropriate to express. During the escalation stage, abusers need to find some rationale or reason to allow themselves to abuse their significant others.

There are two main types of self-talk: thoughts about ourselves and those about others. Thoughts about yourself involve statements about your self-worth or abilities. Thoughts about others may be statements about your partner and his or her worth or abilities.

Identifying and understanding your self-talk about your partner and about those you become angry with is essential if you are to change it.

A particularly troublesome pattern of thoughts is called projection. When it occurs, it is a key factor involved in justifying the abuse. Whatever the abuser does not like about herself may be transferred onto the significant other—this is projection. For example, an abuser may be angry or ashamed of something he has done. Focusing this anger or shame on the victim allows the abuser to feel better about himself and allows a venting of emotions. Another common example involves the disloyal spouse who, ashamed of her infidelity, accuses the loyal spouse of having affairs.

Now that you have a general overview of the escalation stages, we can examine each stage in greater detail. I have compiled tables of common behaviors, emotions and self-talk for each stage. If you are involved in an abusive relationship, remember that these should be a starting point for your own lists.

Stage 1: Normal

This stage is characterized by a healthy, positive attitude. Life appears to be going well and little may bother the abuser.

Behaviors	Emotions	Self-talk
Paying bills	Happy	"I'm doing well."
Relationship going well	Wanted Calm	"People like being around me."
Good general health	Respected	"I do things right."
Performing satisfactorily at work	Competent Trusted	"My significant other wants and loves me."
	Loved	"I am a good parent."

Stage 2: Triggered

At some point, stressors in the abuser's life disrupt normal, healthy behavior. Everyone must face problems such as getting behind at work, slow drivers who hold up traffic and conflict within a relationship. Because of their Low Frustration Tolerance (LFT), abusers do not handle these events appropriately and instead begin to escalate.

Behaviors	Emotions	Self-talk
Yelling	Confused	"Why is this happening to me?"
Sulking	Irritated	"How could he do this to me?"
Avoidance of stressor or person	Frustrated	
Starting arguments	Annoyed	
	Angry	

Stage 3: Victimized and powerless

Frustration makes the abuser feel as though he or she lacks power and control.

Behaviors	Emotions	Self-talk
Pouting	Used	"What am I supposed to do?"
Sulking	Abandoned	"Don't I deserve to be happy?"
Pacing	Betrayed	"How could she do this to me?"
Crying	Powerless	"There's nothing I can do about it."
Refusing to listen to others	Alone	
	Frustrated	
	Cheated	

Stage 4: Anger and depression

As we saw earlier in the chapter, abusers have difficulty identifying and dealing with many emotions. Rather than coping with feelings of frustration, isolation and powerlessness, the abuser interprets them as anger and depression.

Behaviors	Emotions	Self-talk
Raising the voice	Hurt	"He pushes my buttons."
Threatening others	Frustrated	"He has no right to do this to me."
Beginning to drink or take drugs	Excited	"He doesn't love me."
Sulking	Concerned	"I am unlovable."
	Confused	"He deserves whatever I do."
	Angry	

Stage 5: Isolation

Distressed by their emotions, abusers push others away instead of accepting the support they may offer.

Behaviors	Emotions	Self-talk
Sitting at home in the dark	Alone	"No one cares."
Not answering the phone	Confused	"No one would like me if they knew what I was thinking."
Avoiding talking to others	Hurt	"She isn't meeting my needs."
Not participating in group activities	Sad	"I am no good, but I deserve to have my need met."
Breaking off engagements with people	Different from others	"I'll show her."
Being argumentative to get others to go away	Inadequate	

Stage 6: Revenge planning

Unlike the other stages, there are few externally observable behavioral cues that indicate revenge planning. Instead, the abuser fantasizes about and plans behaviors that will soon occur. I have therefore included a list of acts of revenge many abusers consider during this phase. Follow this format as you make your own list.

Planned Behaviors	Emotions	Self-talk
Coming home late without an explanation	Anger	"I'll show him."
Having an affair	Powerful	"He deserves this."
Destroying partner's belongings	Invincible	"I'll have him begging for mercy."
Ending the relationship	Justified	"He'll never hurt me again once I do this."
Misspending money		
Physically or sexually assaulting partner		

During escalation, there is a buildup of tension involving all of the cue areas. When anyone experiences tension, he seeks ways in which to release this tension. In everyday life, this may include healthy outlets such as treating oneself to a special dinner, a movie, a vacation or exercise. But when healthy outlets are not easily accessible, not known or—most commonly—simply not chosen, tension continues to build up until violence may seem the only relief possible. The concept of a volcano is helpful to illustrate the effects of stored tension. When enough tension or energy is ignored, a violent eruption can be expected. The same holds true with emotional tension.

The Explosion Stages

Tim tells Bobbie that she is worthless and pushes her against the wall. Bobbie attempts to get away, but Tim punches her in the stomach. Tim has given himself permission to physically harm Bobbie.

*Betty throws a book at William's picture hanging on the wall,
breaking the frame. Yelling, she accuses him of wanting to end the
relationship. She grabs him by the arm and slaps him across the face.
She then storms out of the house, leaving William hurt, injured, confused and afraid.*

Both of these examples could happen to anyone, male or female.
In both stories, the abuser vents anger inappropriately, causing the
victim to experience harm and fear and damaging the relationship to
a potentially irreparable degree.

When the threshold of tension has been reached and the abuser
believes that enough justification is present, the next stages occur: the
explosion stages. These involve the actual psychological, physical
and/or sexual abuse. The major release of tension occurs, as if a volcano
has finally achieved enough pressure to erupt.

For those who are experiencing abuse for the first few occasions,
the explosion stage may only include emotional or psychological abuse.
This means that the abuser is at the beginning of the abuse continuum.

The major myth involved in the explosion state is that the violence
is uncontrolled, that the abuser has no control once the threshold of
tension is crossed. *But the reality is that the abuser is in total control, the
abuse is not an uncontrolled act and the abuser is able to stop at any time.*

Abusers typically believe that their significant others deserve and
need the abuse, as a child needs discipline—although with much
more force and violence. The abuser thrives on the adrenaline rush
that occurs during violence. The more force the abuser uses, the more
adrenaline is released and the more the abuser feels in control, powerful and excited as the victim is forced into complete submission.

Remember as we examine the stages of explosion that each abuser
experiences the cycle in a unique way. If you are a victim or an abuser,
take time after reading about the common behaviors, emotions and
self-talk to compile your own list of characteristics for each stage as
you did for the escalation stages.

Stage 7: Acting out the revenge plan

The first stage of explosion involves primarily psychological and verbal abuse. During the first few abusive incidents a person experiences, this may be the only stage of explosion. This means that the abuser is still at the beginning of the continuum of abuse described later in this chapter. As the abuse cycle is repeated, this stage will be followed by increasing levels of violence.

Behaviors	Emotions	Self-talk
Coming home late	Powerful	"She will listen next time."
Getting into verbal arguments	In control	"She deserves this."
Playing mind games	Satisfied	"This will teach her a lesson."
Blaming other people		"I am strong."
Neglecting responsibilities		"She won't do that to me again."

Stage 8: Self-destructive behavior

This is a stage of seemingly contradictory emotions, behaviors and self-talk. The abuser hurts the victim by hurting himself. The abuser may genuinely believe that his behavior is out of control, but at the same time feel powerful and in control.

Behaviors	Emotions	Self-talk
Initiating conflicts with authority figures	Confused	"It doesn't matter."
Engaging in sexual compulsive behaviors	Sly	"Nobody cares."
Driving recklessly	Agitated	"Who's going to stop me?"
Neglecting health	Invincible	"I can't control myself."
Not taking prescribed medications	Vengeful	"This won't hurt anyone."

| Behaving compulsively (e.g., overeating, gambling, becoming intoxicated) | Physically and sexually aroused | "It's time for my needs to be met." |

Stage 9: The assault

During this stage, the victim's safety is in dire jeopardy. The abuser has decided that violence is acceptable.

Behaviors	Emotions	Self-talk
Psychological abuse	Powerful	"He deserves this."
Threatening	Vengeful	"He wants this."
Physical battering	Justified	"He asked for it."
Sexual assault	Physically and sexually aroused	"See what he made me do?" "She owes me this much."
Rape	Angry	"He'll never challenge me again."

At this point the abuser's tension has been released. The explosion subsides, to be replaced by misleading pleasantness.

The Honeymoon Stages

The honeymoon stages involve the process of making up after an abusive episode. Apologies may be exchanged and the abuser may even promise never to hurt the victim again. Gifts may be given, extra-pleasant behavior may occur. Calm and communication may return, but never to the same degree as before the abuse occurred.

In his mind the abuser believes that he taught the victim a lesson and that the victim supported the abuse by not reporting it to anyone, as well as by remaining in the relationship.

The abuser may also experience guilt and shame but he may be unsure of how to cope with and express these feelings. The complex, often confusing patterns of emotions, behaviors and self-talk that emerge during these stages are as important to understand as those in the escalation and explosion stages. Although the abuser may seem to be kind and caring at this point, it is essential to recognize that this is still a part of the cycle and that it needs to be changed.

Stage 10: Relief

Having vented anger during the explosion stage, the abuser's immediate reaction is a feeling of release.

Behaviors	Emotions	Self-talk
Making up with the victim	Happy	"Now she will know to please me next time."
Promising it won't happen again as long as the victim obeys	Calm	"It was his own fault."
Telling the victim it was his or her fault	Empowered Satisfied	"I've done what was needed."

Stage 11: Fear of consequences

The abuser realizes at this point that his behavior was unacceptable. Suddenly considering how others, including the victim, will react, the abuser seeks to avoid any unpleasant repercussions of his actions.

Behaviors	Emotions	Self-talk
Giving gifts	Fear	"How can I make sure no one finds out about this?"
Promising it will never happen again	Guilt	"I never meant to do this."
Blaming alcohol or drugs	Shame	"What will my friends and family think?"

| Threatening to harm the victim if he or she tells | Helplessness | "I do not want to go to prison." |
| Lying to hide abuse Displaying unusual kindness and consideration | Confusion | "Never again." "I can't let her leave me." |

Stage 12: Avoidance

To escape the feelings of guilt and shame, the abuser employs various strategies to dodge any responsibility for the abuse. Sometimes he may simply try not to talk about the abuse or to distract the victim with irrelevant issues; in other cases he may make excuses.

Behaviors	Emotions	Self-talk
Changing the topic	Fear	"It was a part of me I cannot control."
Blaming the victim	Confusion	"It's not like me to do that."
Blaming stress	Power	"I would never do that if I was sober."
Claiming to have been out of control	Vindication	"He must be exaggerating what I did."
Blaming alcohol or drugs	Vulnerability	"I don't remember."

Stage 13: Rationalizing

Faced with his or her responsibility, the abuser feels a need to prove that the abuse was fully justified.

Behaviors	Emotions	Self-talk
Arguing	Fear	"I must not have known what I was doing."
Offering excuses	Confusion	"She made me do it."
Defending abuse	Defensiveness	"I was out of control."
Distorting events	Victimization	"It was the drugs, not me."
Using drugs or alcohol		

Stage 14: Victim grooming/Rationalizing the abuse

This is the quintessential honeymoon stage. Having released his or her tension, the abuser feels firmly in control and is willing to be as magnanimous as necessary to keep the victim around. Although the abuser may not realize it, there is still an underlying feeling of fear hidden in this stage. He or she wants to be quite sure the victim will remain locked in the relationship for another turn of the cycle.

Behaviors	Emotions	Self-talk
Giving gifts	Powerful	"He trusts me."
Spending time with the victim	In control	"She wants me."
Showing affection and concern for the victim	Attractive	"This is going to be great."
Arranging for the victim to be dependent on abuser for money or affection	Well-liked Ingenious Fear	"He knows I'm right." "I guess I can afford to be nice now."

Over time, the abuse cycle escalates in frequency, duration and severity. As the Escalation of Abuse diagram portrays (see Figure 3), the escalation stage becomes significantly shorter, requiring less and less time to reach the explosion stage. The explosion stage increases in the severity of violence and becomes longer in duration.

The Victim's Experience

During the escalation stages, the victim feels trapped, helpless and fearful of the impending abuse. He or she may take responsibility for the abuse, experiencing guilt and shame. Believing that abuse is coming as a result of having seen the abusive pattern of behavior before, the victim may provoke the abuser to get it over with or, in order to avoid the abuse, the victim may attempt to appease the abuser. Most often it does no good. The victim may attempt to do whatever his significant other demands, such as performing unwanted sexual acts, confessing to the abuser or others that the victim as actually to blame and so on. The result is degradation, fear and shame.

The victim may attempt to prepare herself for the impending abuse by developing defensive self-talk. For example, the victim may begin telling herself that the abuse is deserved and may make statements such as "If I'd only be less selfish," "She wouldn't abuse me if she didn't love me," or "I deserve this." The victim may also prepare for the impending abuse by disassociation and by assuming a defensive posture to protect his body. *Disassociation* refers to the state of temporarily leaving reality at the time the abuse occurs. It is as if the victim is observing someone else being abused, as if the person is a bystander to his own victimization.

During red flag situations, the victim may attempt to "walk on eggshells" in an attempt to avoid fueling the abuser's escalation energy. To do this the victim may avoid certain topics, accept blame for the abuser's actions or even attempt to leave the situation to avoid being injured. Communication becomes one-sided; the abuser speaks to and for the victim. Again, the abuser hears only what he wants to

Figure 3.
The Escalation of Abuse

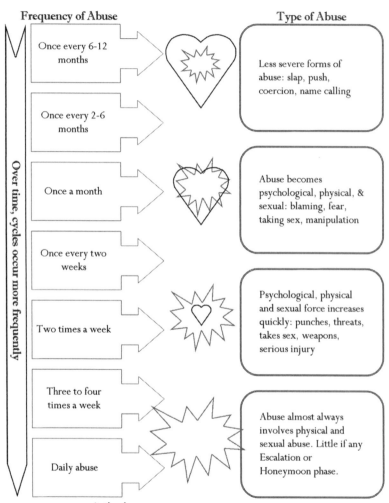

Frequency of Abuse

Once every 6-12 months

Once every 2-6 months

Once a month

Once every two weeks

Two times a week

Three to four times a week

Daily abuse

Over time, cycles occur more frequently

Type of Abuse

Less severe forms of abuse: slap, push, coercion, name calling

Abuse becomes psychological, physical, & sexual: blaming, fear, taking sex, manipulation

Psychological, physical and sexual force increases quickly: punches, threats, takes sex, weapons, serious injury

Abuse almost always involves physical and sexual abuse. Little if any Escalation or Honeymoon phase.

As the abuse progresses...
- Escalation Phase is shortened, taking less time to become violent.
- Honeymoon Phase is shortened.
- Severity of violence increases.
- Violence spreads to others.
- Violence may occur in presence of others.

hear and twists the truth to fit his own twisted sense of reality, which again is part of a self-fulfilling prophecy.

Threats are made and fear increases. Threatening to leave the abuser or to terminate the relationship usually only serves to increase the intensity of the abuse. It is best to leave the abuser and the relationship *without* giving warning.

During the escalation and explosion states, abusers welcome any information, threats or statements that challenge them, because these become the justification for further escalation. Abusers will utilize any excuses they can to avoid taking responsibility for their own actions. It is important to remember that regardless of the actions of the victim, the abuser is always 100 percent responsible for her own behavior and nothing the victim does will lessen the chance of violence happening once the abuser's mind is set.

At times, the abuse may be avoided if the victim gives in to the abuser. But this is a catch-22 situation: if the victim gives in, the abuser's delusional thinking is strengthened, but by not giving in, further psychological, physical and sexual harm may occur. It becomes a matter of survival and any decision made results in the victim losing. Even if physical or sexual abuse may be avoided, emotional and psychological abuse occur. If the victim does give in to the demands of the abuser, the physical and sexual abuse may still occur, although with less severity and intensity than if the victim refuses to give in.

At this point, the victim physically prepares for the abuse and attempts to cover and protect body parts and possessions from harm. The victim may begin to tremble and become hypervigilant of the abuser and of the environment, seeking places to get help or hide. Victims may experience stomach cramps, headaches, neck aches, lumps in their throats and sweating. In this crisis situation the victim attempts to survive the abuse in any way possible.

During the explosion stage the victim experiences fear and injury and feels degraded, often believing that he is responsible for being abused. A sad but common thought passing through victims' minds is "What did I do to deserve this?" The correct answer is "nothing."

The abuser planned how, when and where the abuse would occur and the victim's efforts to prevent or stop the abuse were futile.

Once the honeymoon stages begin, the victim may feel relieved that the present abuse is over and may begin to feel hopeful that the abuse will never happen again. However, most victims have seen this pattern of abuse before and have heard many broken promises. Still, those who remain in the situation feel thankful the abuse has ended, if only temporarily.

Steve and Mary are abuser and victim. They have known each other for several years and have been dating for about six months. Mary was originally seen by a therapist for depression and upon further evaluation her therapist recognized that she was being abused. Mary said that her depression was worse after she and Steve had an argument.

Steve reluctantly came in to see me, making it clear that Mary was the problem and that he was the victim of having to tolerate her mood swings. Steve became angry with me when I asked if he had a difficult time dealing with his anger. I explained that his anger problem had nothing to do with Mary and that he needed to learn about the cause of his anger. Steve gradually opened up and said that when he was stressed and things did not go the way he planned, he became tense and easily annoyed and looked for something to justify venting his anger on her.

We began to discuss the escalation stage. He identified his cues as muscle twitching, neck tightening and aching, narrowing his eyes to focus on Mary, yelling and calling her names and clenching his teeth and fists. Mary added that when issues of commitment or sex came up, he began to distance himself emotionally from her and even to avoid her at times. Steve's escalation stage usually lasted for about two weeks.

Steve's explosion stage involved putting Mary down by calling her a "slut" and a "bitch," bringing up the fact that she had been abused when she was a child, blaming and labeling her and devaluing her

Figure 4

Continuum of Force

Psychological Abuse	Threats	Physical & Sexual Abuse
• Yelling, swearing	• To harm self	• Any physical contact that can or does cause harm
• Name calling	• To harm partner	• Hitting, slapping or punching
• Using personal information to hurt or blackmail	• To harm children	• Choking, strangling, grabbing by neck
• Objectifying	• To harm pets	• Hair-pulling
• Lying/omission of information	• To divorce	• Use of weapon or object
• Driving recklessly	• To spread rumors	• Restraining or blocking
• Criticizing, belittling	• To withhold money	• Talking, pressuring or coercing into sexual contact
• Harassment	• To withhold visitation	• Taking advantage of intoxication for sex
• Stalking	• To assault others	• Using threatening statements to get sex
• Sarcasm	• Displaying weapons	• Using sex to make up or calm down
• Ordering, controlling, commanding	• Insinuating use of weapons	• Physically forcing sex
• Jealousy		• Refusing to accept *no*, hesitations, lack of response
• Explosive anger		• Expecting sex
• Interfering with calls		• Exerting the "male privilege" to get sex
• Limiting friendships		• Tricking or being deceitful to get sex
• Misspending or withholding financial support		

Over time, the intensity of the violence will increase from verbal and psychological abuse to threats, to sexual and physical abuse, even murder.

Figure 5

Continuum of Sexual Abuse

Over time, the intensity of the violence will increase from minor sexual abuse to serious, life-threatening sexual violence.

- Talking into sex
- Taking advantage of intoxication
- Guilting into sex
- Using pornography to deal with stress or anger
- Comparing partner to others sexually

- Pressuring or coercing into sex
- Refusing to accept *no* for an answer
- Tricking into sex
- Unwanted touching or grabbing of sexual areas when in private
- Making unwanted sexual comments
- Openly using pornography
- Repeated requests to view pornography together
- Withholding sex when angry
- Engaging in chat rooms, dating services or internet sites for the purpose of meeting new romantic partners

- Threatening to take sex
- Threatening to physically harm
- Expecting and demanding sex
- Exerting "male privilege"
- Unwanted touching or grabbing in sexual areas when in public
- Making direct, personal, unwanted sexual comments
- Using sexually derogatory language
- Demanding that partner role-play or pretend to be someone else during sex
- Engaging in sexual affairs

- Engaging in humiliating or painful sexual acts
- Physically forcing sex
- Initiating unwanted sexual contact in public
- Engaging in sexually demeaning behavior in private or in public
- Sexually sadistic behaviors
- Torture
- Kidnapping
- Murder

Figure 6

Continuum of Physical Abuse

Over time, the intensity of the violence will increase from minor physical abuse to serious, life-threatening violence.

- Bumping
- Pushing
- Throwing objects
- Breaking objects
- Restraining or blocking
- Threatening more serious physical violence

- Slapping
- Punching on the arm or back
- Throwing objects directly at someone
- Hair-pulling
- Physical abuse in the home or when alone
- Threatening to use a weapon
- Pressuring/talking into sex
- Refusing to accept *no* as an answer for sex
- Taking advantage of intoxication
- Using sex to make up or calm down

- Hitting or punching the face
- Repeatedly hitting or punching
- Using a weapon or object to assault
- Behaving violently when children are present
- Demanding sex
- Exerting "male privilege"
- Threatening physical assault or reminding of past physical assault

- Repeated punching of the head
- Choking
- Using lethal weapons
- Gratuitous violence
- Physically abusing children
- Abusing in public
- Kidnapping
- Physically forcing sex
- Sadistic sexual behaviors
- Torture
- Murder

sense of worth. Sometimes Steve would push Mary against the wall, slam and punch doors and slap her. Mary recalls being pushed on the bed and being forced to have sex with him.

After such an episode the honeymoon stage lasted only for a day or two before the next escalation stage began. Steve would bring her flowers, say nice things, tell her he loved her, promise never to hurt her again and swear that he did not understand why he lost control of himself. Mary would be relieved that this round of abuse was over, but she had seen the cycle before and her sense of helplessness resulted in a growing depression.

The factors most responsible for victims like Mary remaining in abusive relationships are fear and hope (see Chapter 12). Most abusers have a warm, tender side, as well as the hostile, violent side, as did the Jekyll-and-Hyde character. Nearly everyone except the victim sees only the good side of the abuser, which also serves to support the victim in believing that the good, healthy side of the abuser will outweigh the evil, dangerous side. But despite hope, violence occurs again because abuse involves a cycle that feeds itself.

The type of force or violence used also changes over time, becoming increasingly severe, as the Continuum of Force diagram illustrates (see Figures 4, 5 and 6). The chart in Figure 4 shows that there are two types of force, psychological and physical. The types of abuse that occur most often with psychological force are emotional, psychological and sexual abuse. Most abusers begin by using psychological force against their significant others.

CHAPTER 4

Effects
of Abuse

It is extremely difficult to put into words the full effects of relationship violence. Many of them cannot be seen or physically touched, but rather are heard when speaking with victims of abuse. In this section I will briefly examine how relationship violence affects the victim, the abuser, the relationship and society.

The Victim

Victims of abuse often lose the most precious part of life: ownership over one's own life and body. Losing this power is a frightening experience. Instead of focusing energy on the good things in life, a victim focuses all energy on enduring the day-to-day battles that occur as if on a routine schedule. Some victims become submissive, while others become aggressive; both reactions are attempts to survive. Increased medical problems may arise due to physical injury as well as stress-related illnesses.

Not all victims experience the same effects, but those listed here are common. Most victims will experience several of the following:

1. *Fear.* Victims fear many things: the future of the relationship or marriage; financial insecurity; a disrupted home; what others, especially family and close friends, will think if they become

aware of the abuse; loss of safety and security; continued abuse and the possibility of the children being abused at some point are only a few of the concerns that torment victims.

2. *Depression.* Depression sets in when the victim believes that he or she is powerless over the abuser's decision to behave abusively. The only way to regain a sense of power is to hold the abuser accountable.

3. *Low self-esteem.* Victims begin to question their sense of worth and competence with every incident. They often ask themselves what they did to deserve the abuse and, though the answer is nothing, victims have a tendency to blame themselves. An abuser's belittling remarks may also chip away at a victim's self-respect.

4. *Sleep problems.* It is difficult to sleep when you are not able to relax or to trust your partner. In addition, victims may find themselves experiencing nightmares. Other medical problems occur as well.

5. *Impaired ability to trust men or women.* If the victim was abused by a man, it becomes difficult for him or her to trust men; if the victim was abused by a woman, it becomes difficult for him or her to trust women. Victims become used to being abused and if they do not effectively address the issues, they may find that they leave one abusive relationship only to enter another. However, they do not trust again. Trust is a very difficult thing to regain.

6. *Dependency.* Victims may develop an increased dependence on the abuser, especially when the abuser has interfered with the victim's support system, isolating her. The abuser wants this to happen to prevent others from finding out and to increase her sense of ownership of the victim.

7. *Passivity.* Over time, victims tend to become more submissive, tolerating more and more and minimizing the impact of the abuse.

8. *Shame and guilt.* Victims often blame themselves for being abused. Abusers encourage this, doing whatever they can to make victims feel deserving of abuse.

9. *Frustration.* With each lie the abuser tells, with each new sign of the abuser's refusal to change, the victim becomes increasingly frustrated with the abuser, as well as with himself for remaining in the abusive relationship. This may result in aggressiveness.

10. *Helplessness.* Abusers take control away. The abuser makes all the decisions; each round of abuse takes place on the abuser's terms.

11. *Deceitfulness.* The victim begins to cover for the abuser, making excuses to family, friends and coworkers for the abuser's behavior. Over time, she becomes good at denying or playing down the abuse to others. She may also begin to withhold information from the abuser to avoid further abuse.

12. *Suspicion.* The longer the victim experiences abuse, the more likely he is to become suspicious of most everything the abuser says and does. To others, the victim may appear paranoid or unduly untrusting, but abusers give every reason for victims not to trust them and abuse is unpredictable. Paranoia makes perfect sense.

13. *Loss of dreams.* Victims grieve the loss of many dreams. Some must surrender the dreams of living happily every after with their spouses, not being divorced and not having to tell others about a failed relationship, for example.

14. *Suicidal thoughts.* Some victims simply give up, accept the blame for the abuse and attempt to take their own lives. In some ways, this appears understandable: suicide occurs on the victim's terms. Suicidal ideation usually fades as the victim begins to re-empower herself by taking such actions as telling others about the abuse, holding the abuser accountable for the abuse and separating from the abuser at least for a time.

15. *Doubts about competence as a parent.* Victims frequently struggle to simultaneously deal with abuse and fulfill their roles as parents. In addition to trying to protect the children from abuse, a victim may have to contend with an abuser who does everything possible to circumvent the victim's parenting power.

16. *Financial uncertainty.* It is not unusual for the abuser to be the primary wage earner while the victim maintains the household and

rears the children. The abuser may tell the victim that if the relationship ended, the victim would be penniless. The reality is that if the victim was a homemaker or raised the children, then she is entitled to financial support: fifty percent of whatever was accumulated during the marriage belongs to her. Many victims remain unaware of this, however, and therefore live with the added stress of financial worries.

17. *Social impact.* Abusers interfere with victims' support systems, making it difficult for victims to maintain friendships and even straining family relationships. Victims often fear the reaction of friends, coworkers, church members and other people who are important to them if the abuse becomes known. Some people, some churches and some communities condone abuse and blame the victim. The victim may experience direct or indirect pressure from others to remain in the relationship or marriage.

18. *Drug and alcohol abuse.* Victims may turn to drugs and alcohol to cope with the abuse.

19. *Promiscuity.* Sometimes victims will engage in affairs as they search for mates who will treat them with respect, who want to be with them without conditions and who will not abuse them. Although it is not healthy, it sometimes provides the victim a way to compare her relationship with others and may help the victim to decide to leave the abusive relationship.

20. *Risky behavior.* Victims may repeatedly place themselves and their children in dangerous situations to avoid confrontation by abusers.

21. *Doubts about own sanity.* Over time a victim may come to believe that he is crazy. This occurs as a result of others denying his experiences as a victim, especially if they reinforce the myth that the victim deserves to be abused. The victim loses all sense of pride, control and dignity as the abuse continues.

Victims may appear to be hysterical or exaggerating. However, victims' reactions are often very appropriate given the nature of abuse. Who could be abused and remain calm?

The Abuser

Many abusers were victims themselves at one time. They are aware of the humiliation, hurt, fear and pain involved in being victimized, but somehow believe they are justified in abusing their significant others. It is as if they choose to abuse in order to validate their own experiences as victims by victimizing others.

An abuser may hate herself for behaving abusively, but deny she has the power to change, casting herself as the real victim. The abuser thrives on controlling a significant other and may actually encourage the victim to take the blame for the abuse and to feel "crazy." The longer the abuse continues, the stronger the abuser's irrational and distorted thinking becomes.

A shorter fuse, physical complaints, headaches, ulcers and stomach problems may begin to appear due to the abuser's inability to deal with stress; these are symptoms of Low Frustration Tolerance (LFT). Emotionally the abuser begins to experience jealousy, anger and impatience towards others, making others aware of the abuser's problem. Also, the abuser may begin to abuse his significant other in public and may abuse others as he begins to feel invincible, justified and immune from prosecution. Increased alcohol and/or drug use and abuse are also common. The abuser may utilize suicide threats or attempts as a means to maintain control.

The Relationship

The relationship as a whole suffers from abuse. The abuser holds most of the power and relies on violence and abuse to maintain this power, creating inequality within the relationship. Abuse becomes an expected, accepted occurrence. Communication becomes one sided. The victim is neither heard nor respected. The relationship becomes rigid as the abuser becomes increasingly disturbed and paranoid. The couple becomes isolated from others.

The relationship cannot grow and therefore it begins to stagnate. Stagnation leads to a spiraling decline in the quality of the relationship until it finally dies: the abuser is not capable of loving his

significant other at this time. The abuser instead views his significant
other as an object, a possession to do with as he pleases. *Remember
that love has no place for objectification, lust or greed.*

Society

Abusive relationships affect society in several ways. First, if abuse is
allowed to occur—that is, if abuse is not recognized by the community
as a serious problem—then abuse becomes an accepted standard of
behavior. Second, if relationship violence is condoned, then it cannot be
long before any type of violence towards others becomes more common
and, worse yet, accepted. In such a case, society would become more
barbaric. Third, children learn more from observing other people than
by being taught in any other way, so it is clear that abuse has an influence on the adults of tomorrow. Children who witness abuse could
grow to believe it is acceptable, perpetuating the cycle of violence
through another generation.

The Cost of Abusive Behavior:
An Exercise for Abusers

If you behave abusively, your partner is not the only person
harmed. To understand the actual costs involved, examine each of the
following areas impacted by your abusive behavior. Carefully and
thoroughly consider the emotional, spiritual and financial impact of
your abusive behavior in all of the following areas. Be sure to contact
appropriate people to calculate the costs. This may include the court
administrator, clerk of court, police or sheriff departments, hospital
administrators and victim service providers.

Family

Your family has been and will continue to be impacted by your
past abusive behavior and certainly will be impacted by any future
abusive behavior. How has your abusive behavior affected your relationship with each of the following people?
- Your spouse
- Your children

- Your family of origin (including your parents, siblings and other relatives)
- Your in-laws

How has your abusive behavior affected how each of these people views you? In what ways have your relationships changed? Pay particular attention to the damage to trust in your relationships.

Society

Abusive behavior has repercussions for society as well. Think about how your actions impact the following groups:

- Your neighbors: Has your shouting ever disturbed the neighbors? Think about how uncomfortable they may have been, wondering whether they should step in and help or try to ignore the problem. Consider how your relationships with neighbors have changed.
- Local police: Have the police ever been contacted regarding your abusive behavior? How has this affected their view of you? Also examine how their experiences with you may impact the way law enforcement officers deal with abuse in general or with repeat offenders.
- Churches: Many people value their places within religious communities. Has your abusive behavior changed how others in this community regard you? Has it damaged their trust? What effect has your behavior had on how your religious community views violence and intimate relationships?

Financial

Your abuse has cost your family and society considerable amounts of money. Ongoing abuse will certainly increase the actual financial cost. Consider the following categories of expenses:

- Your family: Identify the actual financial cost to your family of your abusive behavior. Include the money paid for fines, damaged property, attorneys, living expenses (if separated) and divorce.

- Law enforcement: Investigation and prosecution of your abusive behavior can be expensive. Identify the actual financial costs incurred for law enforcement services, including the cost of all police that responded to any of your abusive incidents, the detectives' time, transportation and incarceration. Add in any costs for the courts, including the costs for the judge, bailiff, court reporter and any other court-related personnel, costs for attorneys and costs for probation or parole.
- Medical: Costs associated with ambulance transportation, emergency room visits, medical supplies, medications and follow-up services add up.
- Psychological interventions: How much money has been spent on psychological services related to your abusive behavior? This includes the cost of transportation to appointments and support groups, psychological assessments, crisis counseling and therapy services, support group services and follow-up services. Be sure to take into account the estimated number of sessions your victim or victims may attend in your calculation.

Self

How has your abusive behavior affected how you view yourself? In what ways have your credibility and integrity been impacted? Examine the damage to trusting yourself relating to your anger and need to control. As you learn to empathize with the people you have hurt, what feelings do you have about your past behavior and the possibilities of future behavior?

This exercise is not meant to identify all of the possible areas impacted by your abusive behavior but should be food for further thought. Identify and address any other relevant areas.

CHAPTER 5

How Abuse
Is Learned

Abuse is a *conscious* choice. It does not ever "just happen." Even highly impulsive abusers make split second decisions about abuse.

Many factors may influence a person to abuse, although none diminish his responsibility for that decision.

Low Frustration Tolerance

Low Frustration Tolerance (LFT) occurs when a person believes that she is unable to tolerate or cope effectively with discomfort and frustration. As a result of this belief, that person attempts to avoid any situation that might result in discomfort or frustration—for example, not having her needs or demands met when requested, being challenged by others and even the possibility of not being in total control of herself, others and situations.

LFT is a self-fulfilling prophecy: if a person genuinely believes that he is unable to cope with events, he will fail to employ appropriate coping techniques when these events actually arise. His beliefs influence his emotions, leading to behaviors such as avoiding situations in which he may not have the power to be in control, not making needs and requests known or aggressively making needs and demands known. Individuals with LFT also tend to behave impulsively and many choose violence, sex, drugs or alcohol as a means to solve their problems. When a person with LFT is faced with conflict, he will usually seek power and control. These factors make such people likely to become abusive. The stronger an individual's beliefs that she has LFT, the more this person believes herself to be actually out of control and the more abusive she may become.

Power and Control Issues

Power and control issues serve as a primary underlying problem for every abuser. The belief that the abuser needs to be in total control of herself, others and the world is evident when examining the behavior of an abuser and when reviewing the Abuse Chart (Figure 1). Power and control refer to both the desire to have influence over others, such as what they do and whom they see, and the actual state of exerting influence over others—that is, actually making someone do what one wants. Power and control are beliefs that people hold and are maintained by strong but irrational core beliefs. It would be unrealistic and impossible always to be in total control of anyone, ourselves included, or in total control of any situation. But most abusers believe that they should be, and hold strongly to this belief.

An abuser may feel threatened by a partner's independence and desire to have his or her own friends and activities. Control is the abuser's response to this threat. He attempts to make the victim an extension of the abuser rather than her own individual.

When an abuser exerts power and control over a victim, moving through the escalation stages and into the explosion stages, adrenaline is released. The adrenaline may produce a pleasant feeling. It may result in a high, a heightened sense of excitement, like that experienced when riding on a roller coaster. This adrenaline rush is no different from the rush a person experiences when he or she runs or works out. Unfortunately, the abuser may see the adrenaline rush as a reward for abusing a significant other.

Some people become addicted to the adrenaline high and are referred to as adrenaline junkies. When this occurs, they will engage in any behavior that results in the release of adrenaline. Risky behavior, violence and impulsive behavior often provide the quickest and most potent adrenaline rush.

Jealousy

Jealousy is often present when abuse occurs. Jealousy refers to a belief that a person owns something and the resultant attempts to protect the object from being taken away. The primary problem jealousy presents is that *jealousy always refers to an object, not a person*. A person can never own another person and no one can ever "take" someone's partner from her. One's partner certainly can choose to be faithful or unfaithful or to end the relationship, but no one can make him do or not do that. When an abuser is jealous, it is because the abuser truly believes that the significant other is a possession to be owned: the abuser objectifies the victim. Jealousy always leads to irrational, unhealthy behaviors. (Jealousy will be discussed in more detail in Chapter 8).

Jealousy illustrates the fact that abusive behavior is a choice. A person who is concerned that a partner might leave her could choose to remind herself on a daily basis just how important that partner is. Such a person could then focus on giving her partner every reason to remain in the relationship. By expressing love and respect for her partner and making the partner's wants and needs a priority, that person would be choosing a positive alternative to abusive behavior.

These are the three primary underlying reasons that people choose to abuse their significant others. However, there are other factors that may influence a person's choice. It is important to remember that although any of these factors may significantly impact a person's life, they do not cause abuse to occur.

Childhood Environment

Violence within the home ranks as the most important factor in the acceptance of violence in relationships. When children observe their parents arguing and abusing each other, the message the children hear is that abuse is the appropriate manner for the expression of anger or frustration. When children themselves are abused, the lesson is reinforced. Statistics indicate that approximately 80 to 90 percent of abusers and victims have observed family members being abused or were victims of abuse as children.

Other family environments can also be problematic. Chaotic, chronically tense living arrangements in which people rarely take time to communicate set a child up to be neglected. Emotionally uninvested parents may further impair their children's ability to develop healthy identities.

Boundary diffusion, which makes forming healthy relationships difficult, arises when it is not clear where one person ends and another begins. Changing clothes and bathing within sight of others or without closing doors can prevent children from learning appropriate boundaries. Adultifying children with unrealistic expectations by confiding adult information or relying on children for emotional support has similar effects.

Take some time to identify how your family contributed to your decision to abuse, be a victim or develop healthy relationships. For each member of your family (e.g., mother, father, brother, sister and any other significant relative) ask yourself, *What values and behaviors did I learn from this family member that were*

    a. Abusive in nature?

    b. Healthy and respectful?

    c. Confusing?

Society

Socially, violence is reinforced daily. On television and in the movies violence is portrayed as acceptable and, at times, the only sensible reaction to stress, frustration and anger. On the football and baseball fields, hockey rinks, boxing and wrestling rings, violence appears condoned, whether provoked or not. For example, it would be rare for an athlete to be arrested for assaulting another player during a game. Also, much too often when there is a rape scene in a movie, the victim somehow seems to change his or her mind and enjoy the rape, thereby relabeling rape as an act of passion.

To refute these lessons is a difficult job, but it is imperative that we do so. In real life, no one wants, enjoys or deserves abuse—ever.

Laws also reinforce the idea of abuse and violence as acceptable, first by the lack of laws pertaining to relationship violence and second by the level of difficulty often experienced by the victim in prosecuting the abuser. The fact that most athletes and celebrity abusers get off with minimal plea-bargained sentences speaks to the social acceptance of violence. Even when arrested, many abusers spend little time in jail, regardless of the severity or nature of their offenses.

Cultural Factors

The "macho role" and "machismo" foster the belief that men, by nature, are violent and that it is acceptable for men to abuse and/or rape their significant others. This role encourages men to behave in a controlling, aggressive manner. Many men believe that they are expected to be in constant total control of their significant others and that the use of violence to keep them in line is expected. Even today there exist communities where the attitude toward men who commit physical and sexual assault is that "boys will be boys" and prosecuting the abuser is next to impossible.

Difficulty with Emotions

Difficulty expressing and identifying emotions can also lead to aggression. While they may easily recognize feelings such as happiness and sadness, many men have a difficult time with the emotions of jealousy, isolation, anger, love, caring and fear.

Jealousy, which will be discussed in Chapter 8, is an emotion that almost always leads to abuse and is always toxic to a relationship if left unchecked. When jealousy is present, love is absent, because the two are opposites.

Some men have a difficult time being isolated, even for a short period. *Isolation* usually includes feelings of insecurity, inadequacy and abandonment. Men sometimes believe that they must be taken care of by their significant others and that they can not take care of themselves.

Anger, to many men, is equated with provocation, a lack of ownership and lack of control. To be angry is to be justified in abusing others. Anger is one of the catch-all emotions: it is often identified as the emotion being experienced when in fact another emotion, usually one more difficult to cope with, is occurring. When a man who has this belief system directs anger toward a significant other, chances are good that he is really angry with himself and is displacing and projecting his anger onto the significant other, blaming the person for his own miserable feeling.

Fear is an emotion that may also result in abuse, and a person can experience fear of almost anything. For example, an individual may have a fear of losing his or her significant other, of not being a good significant other, parent or friend; of being alone; of what others may think of her; and so on. Fear makes people aware of the fragility of reality, that nothing is ever guaranteed as permanent and that at any time those we love may choose not to be around us any longer. The healthy result of fear, which most people ignore, is that it encourages us to treat others with respect. Fear can help us to remember that our significant other is making a conscious choice to share his or her life with us and that relationships are always changing. Therefore, relationships demand that we change over time and learn to cope with the uncertainty that occurs in any healthy relationship.

Choosing to abuse may appear easier than identifying and dealing with complex emotions. Many abusers use feelings as an excuse to abuse, justifying that if they feel left out or abandoned, for example, then they have nothing to lose and have no other choice but to abuse. As I will explain in Chapter 9, the idea that a situation causes an emotion, which then causes a person to act, leaves out the influence that a person's thoughts and beliefs can have.

Inadequate Social Skills and Support

The lack of any meaningful support network is one of the most important factors in an abuser's choice to abuse. A person with a number of close friends, coworkers and relatives is more likely to have role models who demonstrate appropriate coping and relationship skills. Although some friends and relatives condone abuse, most do not. A social support network outside of the relationship can offer feedback, advice and encouragement. In addition, it is impossible for a person's partner to meet all of her needs. Friends and coworkers may share some of a person's interests that her partner does not.

An inability to establish and maintain friendships may indicate a general lack of social skills. Engaging in meaningful conversation, making and keeping agreements and appointments and fulfilling obligations are important habits in both friendships and romantic relationships.

Mental Illness

Mental illness may increase the chance of abuse occurring because it may affect the abuser's pattern of thinking and reality testing. Examples include paranoia and narcissism, which distort the thinking process. However, this accounts for only 15 to 20 percent of abusers.

Some mental disorders may lead sufferers to behave in self-destructive ways. This may mean engaging in dangerous behavior without regard for injury or something more subtle, such as setting oneself up to lose a job. Abuse may be such a person's way to drive away a partner or end a relationship that was going too well. Although mental illness affects the judgment process, individuals suffering from mental illness often use their psychological disorders as an excuse to continue to behave inappropriately.

If a mental disorder results in an increased chance of violence occurring and the individual refuses to follow the recommended treatment (therapy, support groups or medication), then this individual may need to be institutionalized in a supervised living arrangement or, in the worst case, in prison, for their own safety as well as the public's.

Association of Anger and Deviant Sexual Interest and Arousal

Many abusers rape as well. They may force sexual contact with their partners as a way to "make up" after abuse. To prevent further abuse, a victim may give in to the abuser's demands. An abuser may physically force sex, ignoring the victim's resistance. Sometimes an abuser will rape or even become sexually sadistic as a demonstration of power. He may pressure or force a partner to engage in sexual behavior that the victim finds humiliating, painful or simply unwanted.

In all of these situations, the abuser is learning to connect abuse with sexual arousal. He rewards his controlling behaviors with physical pleasure. This increases the likelihood that the abuser will choose to repeat such behavior.

Relationship Problems Left Unresolved

Many couples do not know how to handle troubles in their relationships. They may marry believing that after the wedding, all of their problems will somehow miraculously disappear and each partner will be a more respectful and invested person. Many couples also believe that having children improves problems.

The reality, however, is that problems and concerns need to be addressed directly when they occur. Even minor issues can grow into ongoing sources of conflict or even power struggles if they are ignored or denied.

Poor Problem Solving Skills

Abusers tend to see things in black and white, as all-or-nothing situations. When compromise is not considered an option, abusive behavior may appear the only choice. An abuser can easily believe his abusive behavior is justified because it offers immediate results.

Some people want what they want when they want it, regardless of how it may impact others. They do not know how to cope with delayed gratification. Like people with LFT, these people believe they are unable to tolerate situations that everyone faces sometimes. Their beliefs about how waiting for fulfillment of their wants affects them are so strong that they think they cannot regulate their own behavior when their desires are not met. They feel as though someone else is controlling their feelings and behavior, although of course this is not true. Such people simply have to learn more effective problem solving skills. Abuse is never, ever, an appropriate problem solving behavior. Abusers can learn appropriate ways to handle their problems and to find nonviolent solutions.

The Struggles of Military Personnel and Police Officers

The significant military and terror-related events of recent years have exposed many people to violence. Let me say this clearly: those who must face life-or-death situations for a living are often heroes. The horrors they suffer help protect the freedom and liberties we take for granted and enjoy daily. These are not bad people. They have often survived hell and need understanding, patience and the trust of others to adjust to their life experiences. They are generally not violent prior to living through their extreme situations.

However, the impact of serving in combat or being stationed away from families can be severe and dramatic and affects the entire family unit. Some of the resulting behavior may include an increase in verbal, physical and sexual abuse. The reasons for this are relatively simple to understand, although abusive behavior is in no way ever acceptable.

One of the realities of war is that people are killed. Military personnel who might normally be passive and nonviolent may, in the course of fulfilling their duty, witness or commit acts of violence that horrify them.

The stressors of combat are similar to those experienced by professionals having to deal with life-or-death situations and crises on a regular basis. Consider for example emergency room doctors and nurses. They may have many people coming into the emergency room with minor, non-life-threatening injuries for days before someone with life-threatening injuries arrives. Yet they always have to be ready for and expect extreme trauma. I refer to this as the roller coaster ride of adrenaline, otherwise known as the fight-or-flight response. Police officers and firefighters experience the same roller coaster. They are always prepared for the life-or-death situations to occur; they have to be ready.

Being ready for such extreme situations takes a heavy toll on the body and mind. Always needing to anticipate life-threatening situations can significantly increase stress and anxiety. Such vigilance may also decrease the ability to utilize healthy coping strategies and even prevent relaxation and sleep.

Even those who are primed to face life-or-death situations may be traumatized by more extreme levels of violence. Consider the firefighters, police and rescue personnel who responded to Ground Zero and the Pentagon on September 11, 2001. They were prepared for fire, for some explosions and for some people to have been killed. What they actually experienced was likely far more devastating than anything they had ever imagined. Their enhanced fight-or-flight responses kicked in and they dealt with the crisis. When the main emergencies of 9/11 were taken care of, though, the police, firefighters and rescue personnel began to experience the aftereffects of such a tragedy. So many lives were saved because of their actions, and yet so very many died because nothing could be done.

This sense of helplessness certainly takes a significant toll on the minds of these professionals, many of whom are used to saving most of the people to whom they respond. Some of the psychological impact on these professionals may have included the following: Some were likely short tempered and unable to sleep. Many reexperienced 9/11 on a daily, sometimes hourly basis. Difficulty relating to family, friends and loved ones was a natural result of such extreme crisis. Some may have attempted to medicate their psychological pain with drugs or alcohol, with isolating or otherwise self-destructive behaviors or with violence. These factors increase the likelihood of domestic abuse and relationship violence among these professionals or anyone attempting to readjust to life following such a tragedy.

Military personnel suffer through similar events and the same impact as they deal with life-and-death decisions on a daily basis. Often stationed away from home for months, sometimes years, they must experience the fight-or-flight response daily during much of that time. They are usually away from their support networks during the time they face the most severe degree of stress they have ever experienced. Military personnel also have little time to process their situation, to adjust to their survival behavior and to cope with everything occurring so rapidly. One cannot fully prepare for the experience of war without having been in a previous war.

Police officers and military personnel have to be willing and ready to kill as part of their jobs, something that very few civilians need ever consider doing. Most never expect to have to draw their weapons in the line of duty and even fewer expect to have to shoot or kill someone. When they are faced with situations that require lethal force, however, it is a matter of survival. Regardless, many have to live the rest of their lives with the memory of having killed.

While in combat, many military personnel are numb to the fact that they actually are killing human beings. I have heard pilots talk about dropping bombs on targets, almost as if they were unaware of the fact that people were killed as a result. Some of the pilots who were shot down during combat revealed how difficult it was to be on the ground and see their targets and to meet the enemy face to face. It can be very unnerving for someone to realize that he has killed many, many people and never once paid attention to the fact that these were human beings. All of a sudden, the feelings sink in as he realizes that he killed to stay alive and so that others could live. This forever changes the lives of police officers and men and women in the armed forces. The experience may result in emotional numbing or an increased sense of guilt and shame. In some cases, having to kill may result in feelings of invincibility and psychopathic beliefs.

Even those who have not had to kill may become lonely and harbor resentment about the military when stationed away from home for extended periods. When at last they return home, they may feel bitter about having been away for so long and may experience guilt, shame or depressive disorders as a result. At the same time, they must readjust to the normal routines of home life.

As much as most military personnel look forward to reuniting with family and loved ones, they are usually also stressed. It takes time to accept that the homes they remember have changed. They have missed many of their families' life experiences and are now somewhat strangers to their own families. Many were absent for milestones in their children's development. Often their family members and friends want to talk about their experiences, but they may not be ready to share such horrors with their loved ones. Such stressors can result in an increase in verbal arguments and eventually lead to abuse.

Returning to a previous occupation can also result in extra stress for which no one is prepared. Many, especially those in the reserves, already had a significant decrease in their monthly pay as a result of choosing to serve in the military. Some may find that their jobs were not saved as promised. Others may find it difficult to return to their previous occupations after serving in combat situations.

It takes even more time for military personnel to let go of the need to be hypervigilant to life-or-death situations and to remember how to behave outside of a war zone. They may resort to what has worked while in combat situations, fighting to win and avoiding vulnerability instead of working things out and employing effective communication strategies. It is to be expected that military personnel experience an increase in relationship and domestic abuse upon their return. It is also expected that many would experience psychological traumas, such as depressive, anxiety and adjustment disorders. Many may resort to alcohol or drug abuse to medicate their feelings and memories of their extreme experiences. Supportive psychological services upon return from deployment or combat are essential for military personnel. Learning how to communicate effectively and to utilize appropriate conflict resolution skills is a must. While on deployment, these people took orders and had minimal contact with their loved ones. They need to reconnect and get used to living their lives as normally as possible.

When police officers or military personnel choose to engage in violence against their loved ones, they are at increased risk for seriously harming their victims. They have the power, knowledge and training to severely injure and even kill. When they become enraged, they may be at higher risk of resorting to these skills. This means that at times, police officers and military personnel may be at greater risk for engaging in child abuse, relationship violence, domestic abuse and sexual assault.

What complicates the situation further is that society has certain beliefs about police officers and members of the armed forces. Concern about meeting those expectations and about the potential consequences of acknowledging they have engaged in abusive behavior discourages many abusers from seeking help. Victims reporting abuse by police officers or military personnel may meet with skepticism and others may not be as willing to hold such abusers accountable.

This attitude works against both victim and abuser, preventing them from receiving the services they desperately need. Police officers and military personnel need to be held accountable just as any other abuser or sex offender would be. Failure to hold them accountable significantly increases the likelihood that the abuse will occur again, usually with more force with each incident. They have the right to have appropriate professional services provided. They deserve an opportunity to heal and to learn appropriate problem-solving and conflict-resolution skills. This can only happen if others hold the abuser accountable and report the crimes of violence. In certain cases the victim may have to contact several jurisdictions, which may include both military and civilian police, rape or abuse crisis programs and police or sheriff departments other than the one at which the abuser works.

Religious Beliefs

Fanaticism can also result in abuse. When a person is rigidly obsessive about a religion—for instance, one in which the man is considered the boss or "head" of the household—abuse is more easily disguised as discipline. Many abusers who are religious fanatics use scripture as a means to justify abusing their significant other or children. The abuser misinterprets scriptural passages and uses them out of context. But the Bible in no way justifies abuse; in fact, it offers several passages against abuse, violence, child abuse, drunkenness and jealousy.

One couple I counseled whose case had elements of religious fanaticism was Peter and Lori. Peter and Lori had been dating for over a year. Peter's parents followed a small, cult-like religion and raised Peter to obsessively follow their beliefs. One of these beliefs was that the man held the power in a relationship and that the woman was to be submissive to his needs and not achieve outside the home. This presented a problem for Lori, who wanted to finish college and was even considering graduate school. Peter flatly informed her that she could not continue to attend college and that she should not make plans to work unless the job was menial and part time.

Peter further told her that she could not spend any time alone with male friends and that he expected her at home with dinner on the table when he arrived. When she was late getting home he would blow up. He frequently intimidated and threatened her and believed that it was all right to punish her for acting in ways that, according to him, only sinners and sluts acted. He was jealous of any male friends she had, although Lori had never been unfaithful to him. Lori was expected not to argue with Peter, even when Peter was wrong and unfair.

Hearing this, Lori became irate. Who was this man to order her around, to tell her which job to work at, or to determine her educational limits? She told him that he could not control her life and that if he continued to treat her abusively, she would leave him. Peter's parents became involved, scolding Lori for talking back to their son. Later, Lori attempted to discuss her concerns with Peter. She explained that her family values were different and that she expected and demanded to be treated with respect.

This was the last straw for Peter. He cursed her, grabbed her by the hair, slapped and punched her and threw her down on the floor, where she lay bleeding. He threatened that if she ever refused his wishes again, talked back to him, embarrassed him in front of his parents or attempted to maintain friends of whom he did not approve, she was "really going to get it."

Lori got the message loud and clear: if she refused to be Peter's puppet and victim, she was going to experience further harm. She left that night and called the police. Peter was arrested for domestic abuse and making terroristic threats.

Lori began to get the support she needed at a support group for abused women. In our sessions together, I explained to her that no one deserves to be abused, ever. It took a while for her to believe me, but she finally did. Peter fought the therapy process. He argued that Lori was to blame, that she was a sinner and that men are supposed to be in charge of any relationship. Peter stated that it was Lori's fault that he had begun to abuse alcohol and that when he became drunk he could not control himself. When I told Peter that alcohol did not cause him to do anything, he became frustrated and quit therapy.

From the beginning, Lori had recognized that something was not right in her relationship with Peter. Leaving immediately after the first incident of physical abuse probably saved her life.

Lori's family of origin had open communication, encouraged the members to achieve whatever goal they were able to and supported each other. It was not a perfect family, just an average family. Peter's family held rigid beliefs, giving no one room for personal growth. Peter became paranoid as his attempts to have total control over Lori failed. His abuse of alcohol increased. The alcohol helped to medicate his loneliness and the only security he felt from others was when he was in total control of them.

Although violence is often learned by observing others, particularly parents who are abusers, this is not an excuse for new violent behavior in adulthood. Unfortunately, thousands of children live in abusive and violent homes. However, most go on to become conscientious adults.

CHAPTER 6

The Role
of Alcohol
in Abuse

Many abusers claim that they were out of control and under the influence of drugs or alcohol when they abused and therefore are not fully responsible for their abusive behavior. Although most abuse occurs when the abuser has been drinking or using drugs, abuse is always a conscious, thought-out decision.

Alcohol is a depressant; that is, from a purely chemical view, it has a relaxing effect on the body and mind. However, for some people, alcohol has a stimulating effect. It can decrease attention to stressors and consequences. Alcohol does not relieve tension. In fact, it can exacerbate anger, rage, depression, insecurity and other dysphoric states. As a person drinks, he or she may feel increasingly depressed, angry or abandoned.

Alcohol use makes it easier to abuse in several ways. It creates an increased sense of agitation. It promotes a fearless attitude and a lack of concern for any consequences of behavior. Because it decreases inhibitions, alcohol use may make it far easier for some people to become violent or reckless. Perhaps most importantly, alcohol use gives an abuser something to blame for his or her abusive behavior.

I cannot emphasize enough, however, that alcohol is not responsible for abuse. Alcohol by itself does nothing to create or cause anger, rage or violence.

To become angrier, escalated and violent requires a significant degree of concentration and forethought. The abuser who verbally abuses the victim must be quick with the right words and put-downs to counter whatever the victim is doing. He or she must think and respond to the victim's behavior. When an abuser becomes physically abusive, he or she has to force his or her body and mind to wake up, become more aroused and then engage in the abusive behavior. This also requires quick thinking, having to adjust the abuse to respond to the victim's behavior. If the victim runs away, the abuser must catch him or her. If the victim picks up the phone, the abuser responds by grabbing the phone and then beating the victim. Clearly, abuse requires quick and somewhat flexible thinking on the abuser's part. Therefore, regardless of how intoxicated or high the abuser claims to have been, she is still responsible for the abusive actions.

Our beliefs about how we will behave when high or intoxicated are referred to as expectancies; these include how we expect to be affected and how we expect to behave as a result. Expectancies are only the way we believe we will be impacted, not how we actually are impacted.

Certain people who walk on hot coals may say that they do not feel the heat. In fact, they do feel the heat; they simply expect to be able to numb their feet and therefore are able to do so. When they experience heat or pain, they relabel the sensation as anything but negative, allowing them to continue to walk. But they are still walking on hot coals and still may end up burning their feet!

If we believe that when we are high or intoxicated we become more violent, then we are more likely to become more abusive. If we believe that when intoxicated we become more relaxed and easygoing, then our actual behavior will reflect that belief instead. Alcohol does not make us one way or the other; our expectancies do.

Much research has been done on how alcohol correlates to violence. Remember that correlating means that there is a relationship between the two factors; it does not mean that one factor causes the other. Some of the following facts are from my own clinical and forensic experience. Other information is referenced.

- There is a strong association between drinking and dating and sexual violence. (Levy, 1991)
- Approximately 75 percent of all abuse and sexual assaults involve the use of alcohol on the part of the abuser and/or victim. The percent is probably higher due to victims blaming themselves or blacking out. (Bohmer, 1993)
- Seventy-five percent of men and 50 percent of women involved in sexual assault were drinking at the time. (Bohmer, 1993)
- Alcohol is a consistent marker for men committing physical abuse. (Levy, 1991).
- When an abuser was using alcohol, he or she was more likely to experience and hear *no*s as *maybe*s. (Swisher and Wekesser, 1994)
- Abusers often make excuses such as
  - "I was out of control."
  - "I was too drunk to know what I was doing."
  - "I do not remember what happened."
- Sex offenders use intoxication as a justification or rationalization for committing sexual assault. (Marshall and Hudson, 1993)
- Alcohol use interferes with normal, moral thought processes. Although alcohol is not in control of the abuser, it does make crossing moral and legal boundaries easier.
- Alcohol use increases the likelihood of tunnel vision, which allows the abuser to become increasingly focused on gaining victim compliance or sexual contact from the victim. In this way, alcohol can play the role of courage for an abuser.
- Alcohol increases the probability of an aggressive response and has a disinhibiting effect on sexual behavior. (Marshall and Hudson, 1993)
- Alcohol increases aggression by making it easier to experience an increase in adrenaline and decreasing attention to disinhibitors and the victim's safety.

- Alcohol minimizes an abuser's guilt and empathy for the victim.
- Victims are more likely to blame themselves for being physically or sexually assaulted when they were drinking heavily. (Levy, 1991)
- Abusers often use alcohol to manipulate their victims into vulnerable situations. Victims are far less likely to effectively defend themselves when they are under the influence of alcohol or drugs.
- Abusers intentionally get their victims intoxicated, often without the victim's knowledge. (Swisher and Wekesser, 1994)
- For dating violence, physical and sex offenders encourage their potential victims to use alcohol and/or drugs by
  - spiking their drinks without their knowledge
  - playing drinking games
  - daring them to drink or get high
  - inventing alcohol- or drug-related initiation rituals
  - creating pressure to fit in or to impress
- Anger, frustration, depression and rejection are risk emotions and commonly lead to the use of drugs and/or alcohol. Abuse or rape may then follow. (Marshall and Hudson, 1993)
- Alcohol and drug use increases the probability of sexually aggressive behavior.

Doctor Veronique Valliere and Reese Lessig performed one study with particularly interesting results. They asked sexual offenders to identify what they expected—that is, their expectancies—from the use of alcohol. The researchers then gave some of the men actual alcohol and the others a placebo, which looked like alcohol but was actually alcohol-free. This allowed the researchers to test how expectancies impact behavior when drunk. Several of their findings are relevant to our discussion.

First, men who believed that drinking made them more aggressive actually became more aggressive when given either alcohol or the placebo, while those who believed drinking made them more relaxed actually became more relaxed. This implies that if the men believed that they would become mean and abusive if drunk, then that is how they behaved when they believed that they were drunk. If they believed that they became more relaxed and easygoing, then they became more calm and easygoing when they believed that they were drunk.

Second, the researchers found that men who either had been given or believed they had been given alcohol were less inhibited in their sexual arousal when viewing pornography. The subjects showed an increase in arousal in response to both non-deviant and deviant stimuli. The impact of the belief that one was drunk was strongest when men viewed sadistic and violent rapes.

Finally, the relationship between expectancies and sexual behavior was stronger in those who needed an excuse for sexual behavior. What this implies is that men who rape may believe more strongly that when they are drunk, they are actually out of control of their sexual behavior. This belief, not the alcohol itself, may lead them to behave as though they were in fact out of control.

The main impact of alcohol appears to be the creation of *alcohol myopia*, or nearsightedness. The drinker pays more attention to the strongest impulse he is experiencing and less attention to other issues that are less important to him at that moment (e.g., the possible negative consequences for the behavior, the impact on the victim or self-consciousness). Dr. Valliere offers this example: those people who are dead set against singing in public will not do karaoke no matter how much they drink. But for those who really do want to sing in public, drinking facilitates the "nerve" and helps overcome the sense of embarrassment or self-consciousness. Alcohol can lower inhibitions and awareness of the negative consequences. After a few drinks, you may not pay attention to the sense of embarrassment if your urge to sing increases. The same is true for rape, abuse, affairs, spending and other behaviors correlated with, but not caused by, alcohol. Your strongest impulse will win after enough alcohol. You become nearsighted to that urge.

After a few drinks, someone who is already angry or upset may give herself permission to abuse or rape. In fact, many abusers and rapists have claimed that they drink so that they can carry out the impulse or urge. Abusers and rapists are also aware of the secondary benefit of using alcohol when they decide to act out their urges or impulses—that is, the decreased accountability that others may place on them for their actions. Others, including the victim, may blame the alcohol rather than the abuser or rapist.

From Dr. Valliere's research, we can draw several conclusions.

1. Alcohol does not cause rape. I believe this can be applied to abuse as well.

2. Those who are strongly against rape or abuse will not rape or abuse just because they are drinking. This is because they had no pre-existing impulses, urges, arousal or interest in violence.

3. How a person is affected by alcohol is really a self-fulfilling prophecy. If the person expects to become violent when drinking, he or she usually will. If he or she expects to become mellow and calm, he or she usually will. The beliefs of the drinker, not the alcohol, influence behavior.

4. For those who already find violence arousing, alcohol use increases arousal to violent material. That is to say, abusers and rapists think of abusing and raping *before* they drink and drinking increases that pre-existing urge.

When intoxicated, it is much easier to give oneself permission to be abusive because of the influence of alcohol myopia.

Alcohol and drug use increases the probability of sexually aggressive or abusive behavior in people with the pre-existing propensity for it. Alcohol never *causes* violence or sexually aggressive behavior. Dr. Valliere asks, "What brand of beer would make me aroused to a three-year-old?" Well, then, I ask, "What kind of beer makes me want to abuse my partner or force sex?" Most abusers use alcohol or drugs, but how the abuser will behave while under the influence is primarily determined by the abuser's expectations—that is, his or her belief about how he or she will act when intoxicated.

I am oversimplifying this research and the results. If you are interested in the more technical data, you can find the study in the reference section of this book.

Problems in Assessing Alcohol and Drug Use in Abuse

It is difficult to determine the actual degree of intoxication of an abuser at the time of the offense. Often the abuser is not arrested for hours or sometimes days after an assault. Therefore, we only have the abuser's word, and sometimes the victim's, on how drunk the abuser actually was. The victim is not always a good source to judge the degree of the abuser's intoxication. At the time of the abuse, the victim was fearful for her safety and therefore may not have been paying close attention to how much the abuser had to drink. Even before the abuse began, the victim was probably not carefully watching how much the abuser was drinking. If the abuser says that she was drunk, what does that mean? Was she feeling "buzzed" or "good," or was she stupidly drunk?

Many abusers claim that they were so drunk or high that they do not remember anything and did not know what they were doing. Consider, however, that a falling-down drunk is not much of a threat. Ask yourself if an abuser truly could have been so "out of it" yet respond to the victim's every move.

Regardless of how intoxicated he was, the abuser still was aware of what he did as he did it. The abuser made a conscious and planned decision to abuse. Though he may have told himself that being drunk was an excuse, even that required a conscious thought.

The truth is that most abusers were far less high or intoxicated at time of the abuse than they claim and even if they were drunk, they should be able to recall most details of the abuse. Claiming not to remember is usually a conscious cop-out. The abuser implies that his or her memory works well enough to deny the victim's version of the abuse, but not well enough to recall exactly all the significant details. That is not how the mind works. A person who so purposively decides what to "forget" could recall the information if he or she wanted to.

A true inability to remember details is actually quite incriminating. If the abuse or rape behavior is commonplace, the abuser may be less likely to recall specific incidents because they happen so frequently. The less the abuser can remember about the abuse or rape, the more likely that it has occurred frequently.

Even an alcohol- or drug-related blackout does not excuse abuse. Blackouts involve the inability to recall what happened in the past, not something that is happening right now. Imagine if someone ran a stop sign while driving, causing an accident. Now imagine that the driver hit his head during that accident and could not recall the events leading up to it. Would impaired memory after the fact mean that the driver had not been in control of his decision to run the sign? Of course not. In the same way, not remembering abuse because of a blackout does not alter the abuser's responsibility for his behavior. Abusers must be held accountable regardless of whether they remember their actions or not.

According to my colleague Michael L. Cesgta, M.D., the treatment of substance abuse has come quite a distance from the old style of "white knuckling" and attending meetings. Medication is also available to help with ending substance abuse. Although community supports including twelve-step programs are a mainstay of substance abuse treatment, we have learned these diseases have a neurobiologic and neurobehavioral component that can be addressed through both psychopharmacologic management and psychotherapy.

Three medications have come to the forefront that can make the process of achieving and maintaining sobriety easier for those with the disease of alcohol dependence. These are Revia, Topamax and Campral. Recently, the FDA approved bupenorphine to ease opiate withdrawal and help with maintenance. In addition, there are many areas of research in treatment of other addiction diseases such as cocaine, amphetamines and others, although these are still in the early stages of development. In summary, many patients no longer have to suffer through the stages required to discontinue substance use and maintain abstinence. A doctor can determine whether medication can help in a specific case.

CHAPTER 7

Emotions
and Abuse

Emotions are the feelings that give quality to life, adding intensity, color and meaning to our experiences. Emotions in and of themselves are neutral, neither good nor bad, healthy nor unhealthy. However, the behavior we choose in response to emotions can be healthy or unhealthy. Certain emotions, such as respect, caring and love, are more likely to encourage us to make healthy behavior choices, while other emotions, such as hate, jealousy and anger, may encourage us to behave in unhealthy ways.

Many people believe that we are powerless to decide which emotions will be experienced. However, emotions do not just happen, but rather are the result of certain beliefs we hold; that is, our beliefs determine which emotions we experience. Beliefs provide a guide that each person uses to interpret and evaluate experiences. For example, if we hold a belief that it is important to treat others with respect, then we are more likely to experience the emotions of caring, respect and love. If we hold a belief that it is important to be in control at all times or that our needs must be met at any cost, then we are more likely to experience the emotions of frustration, jealousy and anger.

Not only do our beliefs help determine which emotions we will experience, but we can adjust the intensity of the emotions ourselves.

This process is accomplished by using the "emotional thermostat," which can increase or decrease the feelings. When an emotion occurs, we can decide what intensity the emotion will be and adjust the thermostat accordingly. If we place an emotion on a continuum, it will be easier to see our options. For example, *love* could occupy the middle ground between *like* and *idolize*.

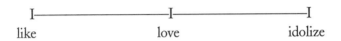

I————————————I————————————I
like   love   idolize

Angry could occupy the middle ground between *annoyed* and *hostile*.

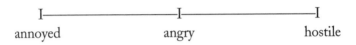

I————————————I————————————I
annoyed   angry   hostile

If we put every emotion on a continuum before we act on it, then we can see the choices we have. If we experience anger and want to act violently, then we adjust the thermostat from *angry* to *hostile*.

Learning correctly to identify which emotions we experience can be difficult. No one is ever 100 percent accurate in labeling all of their emotions. This is not a goal anyone should strive for. However, it is important to be able correctly to identify an emotion that is at least similar to the one we are experiencing, because it is extremely difficult to change our behavior if we do not recognize which emotion is occurring. Often when we behave inappropriately it is the result of an emotion we find to be too painful, frightening or confusing.

The choice when an emotion occurs is to acknowledge and appropriately express the emotion, or to deny, ignore and bury it. It is not always advantageous to express emotions as they occur. In times of crisis, such as when experiencing any type of victimization or loss, it is common and often necessary to deny or repress some emotions in order to cope with the crisis at hand, giving attention only to those emotions of immediate concern. For example, when Dave is abusing Sara by pushing and cursing her, Sara can not safely identify and cope with all of the emotions she is experiencing. Sara has to prioritize which emotions need immediate attention. Emotions such as fear of immediate safety, of being killed or seriously injured, need to take priority. Also, during times of crisis we may not think as effectively as when we are not in a crisis situation, so all the options available to us may not be clearly seen.

Regardless of whether we deal with the emotions at the time they occur or at a later time, eventually we will have to deal with them. Emotions will find some way to be expressed, either directly or indirectly. Coping with emotions in a healthy way involves three steps. Most of the time people complete all three without necessarily thinking about them.

The first step is *identifying* the emotion. Far too often emotions are labeled as either good or bad, happy or sad. We do this because these emotions are commonly accepted by society and involve less risk to express than other emotions. Yet we must correctly identify which emotion is occurring before we can begin to adequately and effectively cope with it. For example, if we are experiencing frustration but label it as anger, we cheat ourselves of the true emotion of frustration.

The second step is *acknowledging and accepting* the emotion, even though it may be uncomfortable, embarrassing or frightening to experience. This allows us to openly experience the true emotion that is occurring. If we do not accomplish this step, we deny ourselves the color and meaning that emotions add to our experience, as well as the right to accept, proudly and honestly, the emotions that occur.

Step three is *appropriately expressing* the emotion. If we are experiencing the emotion of hurt but display anger, two things may occur. First, others may react with defensiveness and hostility, when what we need is support. Second, by acting angry instead of hurt, we do not allow ourselves the expression of hurt, therefore limiting and narrowing the emotions we allow ourselves to experience. To accomplish this step, we must have completed steps one and two and must be willing to take the risk of expressing our true emotions. Learning to follow these three steps takes time, practice and much patience.

Diane often became frustrated with Amy and blamed her for not listening to her concerns. Diane believed that her communication skills were fine, that she clearly identified what she was feeling and that she told Amy about her emotions directly when she needed to. Amy thought of ending the relationship, because she felt that Diane rarely told her how she felt. Both agreed that they argued too much, but neither agreed on what the arguments were about. Diane admitted that she blew up at Amy but could only identify that she felt angry.

Although Amy's ability to correctly label and appropriately express her emotions was not perfect, she was able to communicate fairly effectively. Diane, however, clearly demonstrated to me that she had difficulty with emotions. Diane clearly stated when she was angry but lacked any awareness of other emotions. When Diane was hurt, she buried the pain. When she was scared of losing the relationship with Amy, she became blaming and angry. It took about three months before Diane learned enough about emotions to be willing to explore the emotions she experienced.

Diane learned that when her needs were not met, frustration, not anger, should occur. When this happened and she was let down, she learned to label this as frustration or disappointment. Most of all, when she was scared, this often meant that she was having a difficult time becoming more emotionally intimate with Amy. In the past she would become anxious, tense and angry with Amy, blaming her and even accusing her of cheating on her. This would become abusive when Diane called Amy names, objectifying her.

Now Diane tells Amy when she needs to talk. When she becomes tense and scared, Diane holds Amy's hand and they talk. Diane has learned that only she can control which emotions she experiences and only she is in control of taking risks with Amy by sharing her true feelings. Diane learned that being honest about her emotions was risky, but it was a risk worth taking.

Correctly identifying which emotion is being experienced and which emotion is being expressed involves skill and insight. Ask yourself, "Which emotion does it make sense to be expressing in this situation?" Then name the emotion, acknowledge and accept it, and decide how to express the emotion.

It is also helpful to use the cue areas to help identify which emotions are being experienced. What cues are you experiencing? If you are tense, have clenched fists and a tight jaw, an upset stomach and a red face, then you may be experiencing anger or frustration. These are some of the symptoms of anger and frustration and not all of these symptoms have to be present. If you feel queasy, have a lump in your throat, shaky arms, legs or hands, are teary and try to avoid others, you may be experiencing fear or anxiety.

At times you may find it easier to ignore, bury or disassociate from certain emotions. However, stuffing or burying emotions creates deeper problems, such as increased stress and problems with concentration. Moreover, the buried emotions result in the building up of raw emotion, as with a volcano. The more we stuff and bury, the more sensitive we become to others, sometimes becoming increasingly volatile and sometimes withdrawn. When enough emotion has been stuffed into the volcano (our gut), the result can be an intense explosion of raw emotion, just as a volcano erupts. The emotion released intensifies. For example, if the original emotion that was buried was frustration, the emotion can become intensified and explode as anger or hostility.

Despite the intensity of the emotion being expressed, however, we remain in control of our behavior. Some people choose an easy way out, allowing raw, uncensored emotion to be expressed. The more we stuff, the stronger the explosion of raw emotion, the more severe and extreme the behavior we choose. Such extremes are usually overly passive or aggressive. Someone suffering from depression may turn to suicide; someone suffering from an eating disorder may turn to binge-purging or starvation. In these instances the person turns the violence inward and attacks himself.

When the behavior is directed toward others (projection), abusers often vent their aggression towards their significant others. This is dating and domestic violence. Again the concept of choice applies here, because the abuser consciously makes a decision to hurt either herself or her significant other. When the volcano containing the repressed and buried emotions finally erupts, it does *not* cause a person to behave in any specific manner; the person continues to have the power to choose how to deal with the problem, either by attempting to work it out or by using violence.

When it becomes clear that we are mislabeling an emotion, we have the power to relabel it. There are three areas of focus when attempting to change an emotion. The first is on which emotion we are *experiencing*, the second on which emotion we are *expressing* and the third is on the *beliefs we hold*.

Deciding which emotion we are experiencing appears to be an easy task. Unfortunately, many people mislabel the emotion, leaving them unsure of which emotions they are actually experiencing. Mislabeling may occur for several reasons, including

- A person may be confused and unclear of what emotions are. The most helpful way to overcome this problem is to use a list of emotions.
- Several emotions may be occurring at the same time, which can cloud or mask the emotions being experienced. When you experience a flood of emotions, it is important to ask yourself, "Which emotions are most important in this situation?" If you are having difficulty doing this, ask, "Which emotions should be occurring given this situation?"
- As a defense mechanism, the mind may attempt to protect a person from an emotion which may be too painful or frightening to experience at the present time.

Attempting to identify which emotions you are experiencing can be accomplished several ways. First, you can look at your behaviors: What are you doing? How are you behaving? Are you storming around and swearing or are you calmly talking with someone? Second, you can ask for feedback from others. Someone may tell you that you appear hostile, angry, calm or sad. We may have difficulty observing our own behaviors primarily because we may *think* we are behaving calmly when we are actually behaving hostilely. Others can more accurately perceive and identify our behaviors and we can benefit from their observations. Third, once you have identified which behaviors are being expressed, then you can examine the beliefs you hold that support the emotions and behaviors you choose.

When attempting to change an emotion, it is imperative that the focus be placed on beliefs versus focusing on the emotions directly. That is, focus on the process by which emotions are chosen. Changing your beliefs may change the emotions you experience.

Fear

Fear is a complex emotion that we experience as a result of feeling threatened. Fear represents our awareness that we may be in danger, that things change and that nothing is forever. It may include uncertainty about a relationship, a person or ourselves. Common fears include the fear of being harmed or killed, of losing our significant others, of a relationship ending, of being a bad person or significant other, of looking bad or losing face, of not realizing our dreams (attaining a degree, a vacation, a marriage, maintaining a job), of letting ourselves down, of being alone and of consequences resulting from our behaviors.

Fear can be healthy or unhealthy, depending on whether it is based in reality and whether it interferes significantly with our lives. The healthy quality of fear is that when it is based in reality, it keeps us aware of the need to treat others with respect and to respect ourselves. Fear also prepares us to accept and expect change and growth. Most important, however, is that fear tells us when we are in danger. When fear occurs, trust it—it is usually very accurate.

Anger

Anger often occurs as a result of mislabeling. Anger is the displeasure we experience with something or someone. Although anger appears to be the emotion that leads to abuse, it often represents only a small step on the long road to abuse. Anger is often used to justify abuse—the idea being that somehow the abuser is not responsible for his actions when angry—because society supports the beliefs that anger is the result of provocation and that provocation is enough justification for violence to occur. However, the reality is that anger is a choice; it does not simply occur as a result of provocation. And anger does not cause abuse; abuse is a chosen behavior.

Frustration

Frustration represents our awareness of unfulfilled needs or demands. Frustration may result when things do not happen when we want them to, when our needs are not met to our satisfaction, when we are not able to communicate our needs or wants clearly or effectively and when we lose patience. Frustration can be affected by Low Frustration Tolerance (LFT).

Hope

Hope refers to the belief that things, situations and people can change for the better. Society and religion encourage people to have hope and they foster the belief that people will change for the better if given enough time. Everyone is *capable* of changing his or her beliefs and behaviors, but this does not mean that certain people will ever do so. Again, change involves work and risk; most people will only attempt change when their current behavior is painful, uncomfortable or unfulfilling. Victims may give their abusers the ultimatum that the abuser either stop behaving abusively or the victim will leave. But ultimatums rarely result in changed beliefs and behaviors, and the hope victims hold on to often results in more severe abuse.

Anyone can stop abusing his or her significant other for a short time without help. What helps him or her succeed is the knowledge that after a certain amount of time has passed, he or she may return to the old problem behavior. However, the fact that people can and do stop their abusive behaviors, even for a short amount of time, offers proof that the abuser is always in control of his or her behavior.

Love

Love is the intense feeling of pleasure a person experiences for those people for whom the person cares deeply. Love involves intimacy and spirituality as well as trust and respect, not only for others but for oneself as well. Love is the warm, comfortable sensation experienced when one is with one's significant other, or just thinking of him or her. Love is knowing how, when and what to say, and when to compromise with one's significant others. Abuse and love are opposites; when abuse is occurring, love is absent.

Isolation

Isolation is a real or perceived state of aloneness. Isolation results when an individual is unable to see that he has choices and therefore does not ask for help and support when he needs it most.

When isolation is experienced, it is often due to an abuser preventing a victim from having a support system or the abuser's having been overly dependent on a significant other. Abusers do everything in their power to create the feeling of isolation in their significant others and because of it victims begin to isolate themselves from others in order to avoid further abuse or embarrassment. Thus the victim is without others, without support and alone. Abusers may also isolate themselves by avoiding friends and family and by staying home with their victims as often as possible.

Power

Power refers to the amount of control that abusers and victims experience. Victims experience powerlessness because abusers do whatever they want. Abusers experience power over victims by dictating what the victims will do and even who the victims can see.

Jealousy

Jealousy refers to the fear of losing something a person owns or possesses. Jealousy shows a lack of trust or respect and therefore cannot involve love. We will explore jealousy in more detail in the next chapter.

Confusion

Confusion refers to uncertainty. It usually results when someone is unclear about what another person wants, feels or is attempting to communicate. Confusion may encourage victims to feel crazy or to blame themselves for abuse.

Abusers and victims experience each of these same emotions:

	Abuser	**Victim**
Fear	of losing significant other of losing face/reputation of losing control	of harm of losing dignity of losing significant other of losing security
Anger	misdirected at victim (sometimes) at self	at abuser at self for not leaving may blame self for abuse
Frustration	of unfilled demands, real or imagined	of failed attempts to leave relationship
Hope	of demands being met when first made that victim will remain in relationship	that abuser will change that abuse will end
Love	of self of power	of abuser/significant other
Isolation	from anyone who would not tolerate abuse	from anyone who would expose/end abuse

	Abuser	**Victim**
Power	exerts power	lacks power
	thrives on domination	loses sense of ownership of
	experiences feeling of	body and life
	ownership	
Jealousy	lack of trust and respect	of others' relationships
	objectifies victim	
Confusion	of how to communicate	of why she is being abused
	effectively	of how to get help
	of what he or she really	of her rights
	wants	of her own sanity
	of why victim does not	
	meet demands	

The emotions that occur as a result of dating violence affect both the abuser and the victim. While abusers thrive on certain emotions to help them move through the cycle of abuse, victims may attempt to avoid certain emotions as a way to survive the abusive situations.

Medications can help treat anger and violent emotions. My colleague Dr. Michael Cesta, M.D., says that the treatment of anger has changed dramatically as we develop more of an understanding of its neurobiology and neurobehavioral characteristics. Going beyond the previous methods of individual, group and other therapies targeted at control of anger, we now attempt directly to address anger pharmacologically. Control of anger and other violent emotions is a component of the treatment in many psychiatric diseases. In some instances, an underlying disorder such as depression, bipolar disorder or an impulse control disorder contributes to the development of severe outbursts.

Many medications have been shown to modulate anger. These include antidepressants, mood stabilizers and the new generation of medications called atypical anti-psychotics. Discussing one's anger management difficulties with a psychiatrist can lead to a choice of

medications or combinations of medications which may decrease the
unwanted symptoms of anger, violence and uncontrollable outbursts.
Medications such as Depakote, Tegretol and Lithium are the classic
mood stabilizing medications and have great promise and some suc-
cess of decreasing anger and the violence associated with its extreme
presentation. Even common antidepressants can modulate anger in
certain patients; Prozac, Zoloft, Paxil and others can work to great
benefit in a patient with anger and untreated depression. Some of the
newer medications such as Zyprexa, Resperidone, Seroquel and similar drugs have a broad range of capability and can be very useful in
controlling anger.

CHAPTER 8

Redefining Jealousy

Jealousy is an emotion supported by a rather complex pattern of thoughts. Semantics often create confusion about jealousy, which is generally unhealthy, as opposed to concern, which is generally healthy.

Concern can be viewed as the active part of love. Concern refers to caring for another person. It is the energy we choose to invest in our significant others that focuses on their well-being, putting their needs before our own. Concern is based in reality. A person may experience concern over his significant other's health, job or abusive behaviors. Concern does not involve controlling behaviors.

A relationship based on love and concern is an ongoing process involving commitment, flexibility, respect and honesty—a process that evolves, changes and is challenged over time. People involved in a healthy relationship understand that commitment—the fact that someone decided to share his or her life—is a privilege. They welcome this challenge and are not threatened by the uncertainty it brings.

Envy refers to wanting something that another person has. Envy differs from jealousy in that envy is based on reality. One may choose to cope with envy in healthy or unhealthy ways. Healthy ways involve working for a desired object or earning the respect and cooperation of a person from whom one would like something. Envy becomes unhealthy when an individual allows it to brew. Then it can lead to anger, resentment and jealousy. Over time an individual may become bitter toward the person who has what he wants.

Jealousy and anger are the emotions that abusers most often admit to experiencing and most often use to justify violence. Jealousy refers to the state of suspecting rivalry or infidelity. It implies ownership of something. When a person tells her partner that he cannot do something or see certain people, she is controlling him as if he were an object or possession she owned. When the security of ownership is threatened, a person may respond by becoming angry and fearful about the potential loss. However, most abusers do not correctly identify and label the fear, only the anger, which fuels the jealousy.

In general, emotions are neutral, neither healthy nor unhealthy; it is how we choose to behave as a result of an important emotion that can be unhealthy. Jealousy is the exception to the rule. When jealousy is expressed toward a significant other, it results in abusive behavior. Jealousy is unhealthy. This is due to the mistaken beliefs that support jealousy.

Jealousy involves the fear of losing something, of having something taken away. As I have said before, *a prerequisite to losing something is owning it and no person can ever own another human being!* Jealousy implies a perceived power imbalance.

For example, Paul attempts to prevent Valerie from spending time with others, especially her male friends. Paul automatically assumes that she is engaging in sexual intimacies with her friends simply by the fact that she spends time with them. In order to prevent her from maintaining any source of support, as well as to eliminate any competition for her, Paul does everything in his power to prevent or sabotage any relationship Valerie establishes. He twists the truth to fit his delusion that Valerie is having an affair. However, the delusion is Paul's belief that he owns Valerie.

Jealousy almost always results in inappropriate and abusive behavior. Jealousy deteriorates relationships. If a person views his partner as a possession, the jealous person is not respecting the partner.

It is important to compare jealousy and concern so that the differences can be seen and appreciated. The primary difference is that jealousy is the belief that a person owns the significant other whereas concern is expressing the reality that the significant other may choose to end the relationship, being aware that life offers few guarantees.

Jealousy	Concern
Based on irrational thoughts. Involves cognitive distortions. Misperception of data, of other's intentions.	Based on reality; uses rational thoughts. Thoughts and beliefs based on accurate data and interpreted by beliefs based in reality.
Domination: one is up, one is down.	Equal power: decision-making is shared.
Fears losing significant other, usually based on misperception.	Fears but accepts that significant other may want to end relationship.

The process of how people develop jealousy is illustrated in Figure 7. The abuser believes that he owns his significant other, that the other person belongs exclusively to the potential abuser. Statements such as "He is mine" and "She belongs to me" may occur with jealousy, demonstrating these beliefs.

The second stage is fear. This may include the fear of losing the significant other (either by the person choosing to leave or by someone stealing him away) and fear of the relationship ending. Common examples of self-talk and statements that may occur here include "She is looking to meet someone else so she can leave me" and "That person is trying to take my significant other from me."

The third stage is feeling threatened. During this stage there is an attempt to maintain power and control over the partner due to a perceived threat of loss. It may be perceived that someone else is interested in and is going to attempt to steal the significant other or that the significant other is looking for somebody else. The basic thought going on at this time is to maintain and protect the possession, the significant

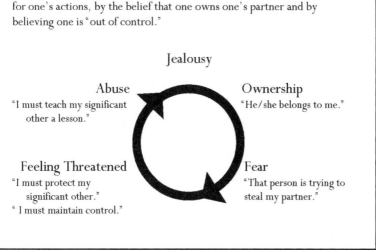

Figure 7—The cycle of jealousy is perpetuated by not taking responsibility for one's actions, by the belief that one owns one's partner and by believing one is "out of control."

Jealousy

Abuse
"I must teach my significant other a lesson."

Ownership
"He/she belongs to me."

Feeling Threatened
"I must protect my significant other."
" I must maintain control."

Fear
"That person is trying to steal my partner."

other. This may include restricting where the significant other goes and who he or she sees. Examples of self-talk and statements that may occur here include "I must protect my significant other," "She is naïve and needs to be protected from being taken advantage of by someone else," "I need to use whatever it takes, including force and physical violence if necessary, to keep her," "She asked for and deserves to have me keep them in line," "She must be punished and taught a lesson if she tries to leave me," and "I need to show her how much I care." In such cases the abuser confuses object love with person love.

At this point the abuser is so fearful of losing the significant other that she believes that abuse is the only way to prove how much she loves the victim and the only way to keep the victim. In this stage the abuser develops a plan of action for the abuse. The abuser plans what to say, when and how to say it, and considers how to act. Plans can involve hours, days or even months of plotting and scheming, or may be made in only a few seconds. The stage is then set for the abuse to occur.

The next stage is the actual abuse. The abuser may use verbal, psychological, physical and/or sexual abuse at this point in an attempt to maintain control over the significant other. The abuser has talked himself into feeling justified in using violence to maintain control over the significant other. Thoughts such as "She asked for this," "She misbehaved and must be taught a lesson," and "I wouldn't do this if I did not love her" may occur. From this stage the process begins all over again.

The abuser may make comments such as "See what you made me do," "I'm sorry, but I lost control," and "I love you so much that I don't want to lose you." These are all signs indicative of abuse involving jealousy. The jealousy cycle is perpetuated by irrational thinking and will continue to occur because it feeds on itself without accepting new data. Every emotion involves a similar process of developing supporting beliefs before the emotion occurs. However, most emotions are based on rational, not distorted, thinking.

Developing a specific belief system requires hard work. The first step is to name what one wants to believe. For example, in order to "own" a significant other, a person must believe that the significant other is an object to be owned and then believe the abuser actually owns the person.

Step two is the development of support for the belief. When support comes from reality, it is often sound. When support for a belief is not based on reality, however, it is referred to as a delusion. Delusions are strongly held beliefs that persist despite evidence that proves them wrong. If a person is experiencing the emotion of jealousy, then he or she is having irrational thoughts that support jealousy. However, that person still remains in control of his or her behavior.

It is important to understand that jealousy does not cause abusive behavior; rather, an abuser chooses to use jealousy as a justification for committing abuse. *No one controls you and no one can provoke you into action. How you respond is always your choice.* Most people have difficulty dealing effectively with jealousy, but that does not justify using jealousy as an excuse for abuse.

The story of one woman whom I counseled illustrates how jealousy affects the victim. Pat often became upset when Leslie spent time with her friends. Leslie had had these friends for many years and spent time with them at least twice per week, usually when Pat was working or out with his friends. Pat yelled at Leslie when she had been with her friends and called her a whore, a slut and a bitch. He told her that he knew her male friends all wanted to have sex with her and that none of her female friends liked him.

Leslie offered to bring him with her when she went out with her friends, but he usually refused. When he did go along, he was possessive of her, not allowing any of her male friends near her. He even threatened one of her male friends whom she wanted to hug.

Things worsened when they were alone. When she refused to have sex with Pat, he accused her of having affairs. No matter how she explained to him that her friends accepted that she was dating him and would never ask for sex from her, he ignored her. He called her a liar and denigrated her until she doubted her own sanity.

Pat told Leslie, "You're mine. No one will want you if you see your male friends again; I'll make sure of that." Leslie was frightened and confused; she had not been unfaithful to Pat. She tolerated his abusiveness and even stopped spending time with her male friends, but nothing satisfied Pat. Not only did he not believe that Leslie was not seeing her male friends anymore, but he also demanded that she not spend time with her female friends. Leslie was expected either to be with Pat or to wait at home until he called or came over. He made it clear that she had better listen and do what he wanted or he would end the relationship.

Pat had stolen Leslie's self-esteem. She gave him her time, her money and sex. She believed that to lose the relationship would be to lose the only sense of worth, value, and belonging she knew.

Eventually Pat began to physically abuse Leslie. He grabbed her by the arm, forced her to listen to him and humiliated her when alone and in public. He even began to rape her, forcing her to have sex with him upon demand. He put her down for not sexually pleasing him.

He blamed her, objectified and sexualized her, and became paranoid and obsessed with her. Leslie was in danger and unable to see any source of help that could save her. Her depression grew, as did her suicidal thoughts. On her fifth try at suicide, she almost succeeded. It was in the emergency room that help finally reached Leslie.

The doctor who resuscitated her was concerned about Leslie's emotional health and sent for the chaplain and the social worker. They told Leslie she was a victim of dating violence, explaining that she had worth as a person and that she did not deserve to be abused. After leaving the hospital, Leslie became connected with a support group for victims of abuse and she began therapy with me as well. In therapy she learned that she had much to offer herself and others, and with support from both her old and new friends, she succeeded in putting her life together—without Pat.

CHAPTER 9

The Role
of Cognitions

*"I really hit the ceiling when you talk about my ex-wife," John,
a short, paunchy forty-year-old, said to his new wife, Linda.*

Often we hear people complain that something or someone caused them to experience a certain emotion or caused them to behave in a particular manner. The implication is that situations and other people control our feelings and behaviors. According to such a theory, we cannot choose what to feel or how to react to others.

Albert Ellis, the founder of Rational Emotive Therapy (RET), strongly disagrees with that theory. He believes that we control our emotions and behaviors and that others cannot control us. Ellis developed a working model to illustrate how cognitions really work. This model is referred to as the ABCs. The intricate details of the ABCs of RET are complex, but understanding the basic principles should be of help in defining irrational thoughts.

A refers to the activation event or situation one is responding to or being affected by. This may be a confrontation with another person or something not turning out the way one desired.

B refers to our belief system, which is the most important component in controlling our emotions and behaviors. We use our belief system to evaluate and give meaning to events based on the values and morals that make up our belief system. Beliefs are our guide to interpreting data and events. Beliefs affect how we choose to adjust the emotional thermostat.

C refers to the emotions we experience following the activating situation. Based on the emotional response, we choose how we will behave.

The most important and often overlooked part of this model is B. It is common for people to believe that they move from A to C. They believe that the event caused their emotional or behavioral response to occur.

Most, if not all, abusers believe that A (situation) causes C (emotion), which in turn dictates which behaviors occur. This belief leads to the irrational conclusion that the abuse occurs simply as a result of an emotion and that abusers are unable to control their behavior (see Figure 8). Holding this belief, abusers begin to feel that their abusive behavior is out of their control.

If this were true, every time the abuser experienced the same situation it would result in the same emotion and the abuser would behave in exactly the same manner each and every time. For instance, John is an abuser who is prone to violent behavior. If we accept this theory, every time John experienced anger he would become violent toward whoever was accessible. In various situations, John would become violent toward his boss, other family members, friends, co-workers and strangers. Yet this isn't true for either John or other abusers. Most abusers only attack their significant others. This offers one proof that abuse is a controlled, planned act in which the abuser chooses to engage.

What was not taken into account here in our theory of John's behavior is the belief system (B). A belief system allows us to analyze a situation and react with a particular emotional and behavioral response. This is how it works: A situation happens (A), our belief system (B) evaluates and analyzes the data and then, based on our beliefs, an emotion (C) occurs. When this happens, we choose the

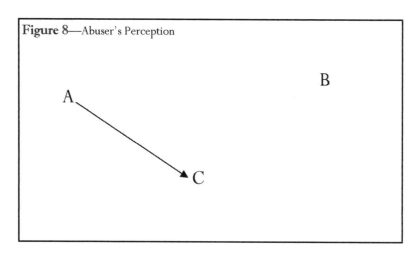

Figure 8—Abuser's Perception

degree of emotion that will be experienced by adjusting our emotional thermostat. Adjusting the thermostat to the desired intensity, we choose a behavior to express that degree of that emotion (see Figure 9).

If there are certain situations with which we continually have difficulty dealing, we may choose to avoid these situations if possible. However, we may not always be able to do so. There are two types of *A*s: those we can change and those we cannot. When certain situations create problems with our beliefs, or when something or someone challenges or threatens our beliefs, we can choose to avoid these situations or people or modify or change our belief system that pertains to these specific situations, thereby offering ourselves different choices to which we may respond.

For example, Jane hates visiting her stepmother, who is overly critical. Jane tries to avoid going to her father and stepmother's house. Like Jane, if visiting a certain person creates problems for us by challenging our beliefs, then we could choose not to be around that person. However, some situations we cannot control. Examples for Jane included her father's serious illness. She could have avoided going to her father's house in this situation, but the thought that her father might die and she wouldn't see him was enough to make her visit.

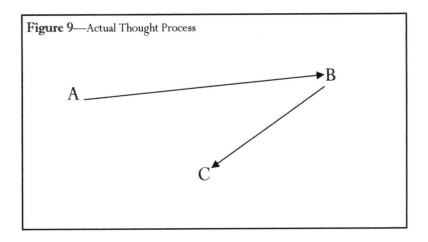

Figure 9—Actual Thought Process

Like Jane, we cannot change or avoid all unpleasant situations. Therefore, we may modify or change our belief system. Changing or modifying our beliefs may allow us to cope with unpleasant as well as pleasant situations in a healthy manner (see Figure 10).

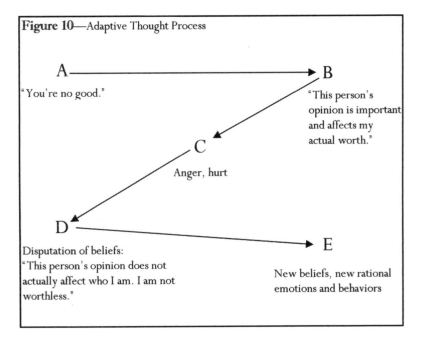

Figure 10—Adaptive Thought Process

There are two kinds of beliefs, rational and irrational. Rational beliefs are true and result in moderate emotions and behaviors. They help us attain our goals. When we experience stress in relation to a situation and our beliefs are rational, the stress level would probably range between the 30 percent and 70 percent level, a range well within normal limits.

0%   30%   50%   70%   100%

Irrational beliefs are not true and result in extreme ranges of emotions. They are based on erroneous and irrational data. They prevent us from attaining our goals and are often commands or absolute in nature. In *A Practitioner's Guide to Rational Emotive Therapy*, authors Susan R. Walen, Raymond DiGiuseppe and Richard L. Wessler explain that irrational beliefs fall into four categories.

The first category contains *awfulizing* statements. Examples include "It is awful when you do not meet my needs" and "It is awful when things do not go the way I want them to." This is also referred to as *catastrophizing*. We can only believe that something bad will happen and we blow things out of proportion.

The second category contains "should," "ought" and "must" statements. These absolute statements dictate that a specific course of action needs to occur and there is no room for other choices. This is black-and-white, either/or thinking. There is no room for any middle ground or "gray" area and as a result a person must choose between two extremes.

The third category includes *need statements*. Abusers often confuse desires with true needs, resulting in erroneous beliefs about what their needs truly are. The reality is that we need very little in life. Food, water, shelter and clothing may be real needs we have, but companionship and relationships are also needs. However, we do not need to have sex whenever we become sexually aroused; reality has proven that if our requests are not met immediately we will still survive.

The fourth and last category includes beliefs concerning human worth. Often abusers and victims doubt their self-worth or the worth of their significant others. Statements such as "You're no good because…" are typical of the attitudes held by abusers and victims. When worth is conditional, dependent on how one behaves, that in itself is abusive and irrational. All people are worthwhile regardless of what they choose to do or not to do.

Three characteristics apply to irrational beliefs: a philosophy of self-denigration (putting oneself down), Low Frustration Tolerance and blaming and condemning others. Some irrational beliefs may include more than one characteristic.

Irrational beliefs are maintained by self-indoctrination—that is, focusing on the irrational belief—and may even reach the extreme of obsessing over the belief, as well as telling ourselves repeatedly that these irrational beliefs are true.

Cognitive Distortions

Cognitive distortions refer to faulty thinking. Most people at some time in their lives use distortions in thinking in order to see and hear what they want to. These distortions also serve to vindicate certain behaviors, especially when these behaviors are abusive. Cognitive distortions include the following:

- *Polarized thinking* is seeing things as all or nothing, black or white, with no middle ground. This is also referred to as absolutist thinking. Either things are going great or they are terrible. For example, our significant other either loves us totally or does not care for us at all.
- *Overgeneralization* is making mountains out of molehills. It involves taking whatever is happening in a certain situation and generalizing to all situations. For example, if our significant other hurts or disappoints us, we believe that all people we trust and care about will also hurt and disappoint us.
- *Thought screening* is seeing and hearing only what we want to and disregarding the rest. For example, if our significant other

had a problem keeping the plans for a date and explained that he or she would be late or unable to show up, all we focus on is how he or she affected us; we disregard the reasons for the changed plans, even though the explanation might be legitimate. All we seem to hear is that the person canceled the date and that our wants were not met.

- *Discounting* is similar to thought screening. Anything positive that happens is minimized and we prepare for an imagined or expected negative reaction. For example, if our significant other gives us a gift, we assume that something must be wrong—that they must have cheated on us or want to end the relationship; if they give us a hug, we may tell them that it meant nothing. Discounting is similar to *minimization.*

- *Minimization* involves underestimating something or someone, not giving credit when credit is due, expecting too much and never being satisfied with what a person gives. Let us say we receive a gift from our significant other and complain that it is only a piece of silver jewelry when we wanted gold; or at a party we cause him or her to feel less important than our friends, the event or something else. Minimizing can involve never accepting what our significant other offers, as if the person owes us so much more when in fact they are offering a lot. For instance, Joelle expected many expensive gifts at Christmas and only received two or three inexpensive ones; she spent the day pouting. Minimizing the meaning of what a partner says because of high expectations would be another example.

- *Exaggeration* is blowing things out of proportion, giving more meaning to something than is warranted. For example, if a partner gives us a gift or invites us to a dance, we might assume that this means she or he wants a deeper relationship, when in fact the person may simply enjoy spending time with us. We gave too much meaning to their behavior. Another example would be to become irate with a partner when he or she tells us they have to cancel plans. To the person who exaggerates, the issue is paramount, when in reality it may be insignificant.

- *Snap judgments* involve making assumptions and decisions without considering the facts or without taking time to think about how to react. An example would be seeing our significant other with another man or woman and assuming the two are having an affair. The reality may be that the person was innocently having coffee and talking, but we come to a decision without asking for clarification. Snap judgments are not based in reality and we had no evidence to back them up.

- *Emotional reasoning* involves interpreting a situation based on an emotional reaction or feeling. For example, if we had a good day at work, we might believe that we must be a good person. If we have an argument with someone and are feeling angry and sad, we feel we must be a bad or worthless person. If we are sexually aroused, we may believe that our significant other is also sexually aroused simply because we are. This type of reasoning involves using emotions to decide who a person is and what the person's worth is.

- *Absolute statements*, or imperatives, are unrealistic demands and expectations. They use the words "should," "ought" and "must." They are setups for failure, because they can seldom be met and are often irrational and unfair to impose on anyone. For example, if we believe that our significant other "should" have sex and she or he refuses, we become angry and feel let down. It may even appear to be a devastating letdown because of our unrealistic demands and beliefs. To believe that "it would be nice if he had sex with me" is a healthy replacement for the "should" belief because it allows our partner to say no without feeling as if he or she has caused a major catastrophe.

- *Labeling and mislabeling* involve objectifying our significant others or ourselves. For example, Mary sometimes wanted to be intimate with Ted but did not desire to have intercourse.

Ted called her a "tease" when this occurred, thus objectifying Mary. Other examples include racial, religious or sexual put-downs, all of which take away an individual's identity.

- *Personalization* involves an assumption that things happen because of us or that others are always referring to us. For example, our significant other ends the relationship with us and we believe that we caused her or him to leave. The reality, however, is that we may have influenced the person to leave, but we did not make the individual leave. Another example is hearing two people talking and noticing them looking in our direction several times; we assume they must be talking about us when in fact they were simply looking at the clock behind us.

- *Rationalizations* are excuses used to justify behaviors. Telling ourselves that we have spent so much money and time with a significant other that she or he now owes us sex is one example of rationalization. Another common rationalization is believing we are out of control, which is never the case. Rationalizing involves finding excuses and reasons that support our decision. However, we always have the power to make a decision. Whether this decision is to back off, to fight, to brutalize or to rape, it is in our power to decide.

All of the above are types of cognitive distortions. Though abusers often use such thinking to justify or excuse abuse, they are never excuses.

Distorted thinking can damage a relationship as well as self-esteem. At some times everyone uses cognitive distortions to cope with situations; however, we must pay attention when we use them. If a person's primary method of problem solving is using distorted thinking, then that person is in need of education and therapy to learn healthy problem-solving skills.

To demonstrate how cognitive distortions can damage relationships and increase the power of abuse, let us look at one couple: Tom and Jim.

When Tom became stressed, he quickly became irritable and frustrated. He had a short fuse and at times seemed almost to beg people to argue with him. Jim recognized Tom's escalation pattern very well, having been involved in a relationship with him for over two years. In a tense mood, Tom would criticize. When really stressed, he would challenge Jim's love for him.

Tom carefully screened everything Jim said to him. When he found the smallest inconsistency, he blew it up, making it into a major issue. One day Jim had spent the morning with his mother, gone to see a friend named Greg in the afternoon and met several friends in the evening. It was his night away from Tom and Tom's night for bowling. When they got together Tom was livid. "You spent the whole day with Greg," Tom shouted. "You would rather be with Greg than with me."

Jim sighed. "On one hand, this is true, because Greg treated me with respect, but I'm really faithful to you."

In my therapy session with Tom and Jim, Tom continued to hear only what he wanted to and discounted much of what Jim said. Jim wanted to resolve his issues and to improve and save the relationship. Tom also wanted to save the relationship, but minimized any responsibility for their problems. It took several sessions before both agreed that their relationship was abusive and that Jim was the victim. Tom reluctantly accepted that the way he treated Jim was verbally and psychologically abusive. Interestingly, Tom stated that his father would often put his mother down and would belittle any accomplishment Tom or his siblings made. His father expected everyone to jump through hoops before getting any sort of acceptance or approval.

Tom was badly trained by his father and chose to continue the cycle of abuse in his own relationships. In our sessions, Tom learned to listen to what was being said, to hear the message before responding. This helped him recognize how he had twisted the messages from Jim to fit what he wanted to hear. He was surprised at how good it felt to really listen and hear Jim's messages. Jim learned how to let

Tom know when he was not listening by telling Tom to stop and let Jim finish or restate his message.

The relationship between Jim and Tom showed other signs of victim and abuser roles that had to be worked on. Tom stereotyped men to be provocateurs of abuse; this came from his father mostly blaming the abuse in their childhood home on Tom. Tom viewed Jim as an argument waiting to happen, somehow always deserving to be put in his place. As our meeting progressed, Tom finally understood that he had learned to be abusive from his father. He felt relieved that he wasn't born an abuser. Most importantly, Tom learned that he could change the way he viewed women and men and make a conscious effort to empower Jim instead of taking power away from him.

CHAPTER 10

Relationships and Abuse

We all search for that special someone to share our lives, someone with whom to share our dreams, successes and failures. Yet many people have not yet developed and matured as individuals, which is a prerequisite to becoming constructively involved in any relationship.

Relationships serve several purposes, including friendship, advice, companionship and romance. Some people hold the belief that a single person can fulfill all of a person's needs for affiliation. If we expect our significant other to fulfill the roles of friend, confidant, advisor and so on, this is a difficult, perhaps impossible, demand to carry out. To impose it on one person may deeply frustrate that individual.

Other consequences of having these unrealistic expectations may include irritation, arguing, increased distance between partners and unhealthy communication. Often the result is an unhealthy relationship. The couple ends up further apart, while emotionally clinging to each other at any cost, because to lose each other would result in aloneness and isolation.

Most people do not fully understand what a relationship is, nor do most people truly understand what to expect from others or how to treat others. This chapter is in no way intended to serve as an in-depth guide to relationships, but rather as an overview of what a relationship is and what it requires from each person, and to describe and contrast healthy and unhealthy relationships.

The most important aspect of any relationship is that it is a fluid, ever-changing interaction and exchange of affection and energy. No relationship is guaranteed to be permanent. Each person must continually work at maintaining it. A relationship is an intimate, romantic, passionate attachment between two people. A relationship has three identities: *me, you* and *we.* Together the three form a triangle.

Figure 11 illustrates what a healthy relationship looks like. Each of the identities devotes energy to the well-being of the other identities. Each also receives the investment of energy from the others. A healthy relationship demands that all three identities are separate and each be allowed to grow. Each identity should have clear boundaries. Remember that a relationship is always changing; therefore, each person or identity should be allowed to grow individually and independently, as well as to grow closer together. All identities are equal in a healthy relationship. Not only can a healthy relationship withstand having others involved, but it *demands* the involvement of others.

Unhealthy relationships are illustrated in Figures 12 and 13. When a relationship is unhealthy, neither person dares to be separated from the other for any amount of time out of fear of losing or

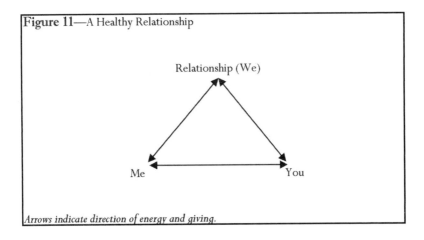

Figure 11—A Healthy Relationship

Relationship (We)

Me   You

Arrows indicate direction of energy and giving.

sacrificing the small amount of self-identity each has managed to hold to. It is as if their individual identities are so fragile that they believe they may disintegrate without the other person. Both people are dependent on the relationship and afraid to jeopardize it.

In Figure 12, the relationship consumes each person's identity. Both people give up their dreams, goals and individuality and eventually become consumed by and trapped in the relationship. People who center their lives on the relationship, who do not have a separate identity or support network, are commonly in this type of relationship.

In Figure 13 the relationship centers on the demands and requests of one person. Abusive relationships almost always look like this—a one-up and one-down situation where the focus of the relationship is on maintaining a tenuous equilibrium and the only way to do this while maintaining the fragile relationship is to be a victim.

Abusers believe that their significant others are around to meet any and all of their demands in exchange for not psychologically, physically or sexually harming the significant others. The abuser dominates both the significant other and their relationship. As time passes the abuser will grow ever more domineering and controlling over the victim and nearly always believe that he owns his victim.

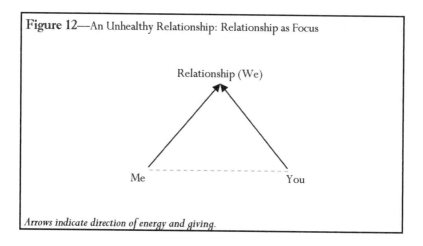

Figure 12—An Unhealthy Relationship: Relationship as Focus

Relationship (We)

Me   You

Arrows indicate direction of energy and giving.

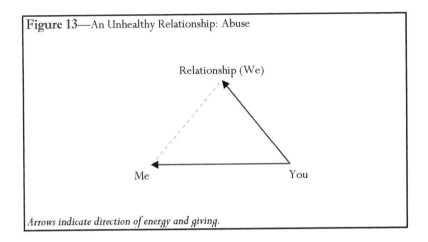

Figure 13—An Unhealthy Relationship: Abuse

Relationship (We)

Me   You

Arrows indicate direction of energy and giving.

Because of the belief that they own their significant others, abusers tend to view the time with their victims as being "spent" rather than "shared" with them.

There is a major distinction between the two. *Spending* implies having something and exchanging it for something in return. When a person spends time with someone, it is as though he gives something up and exchanges it for something else. The idea of spending time with a significant other results in an empty form of intimacy. Love cannot be bought.

Effectively *sharing* a life with someone involves a non-possessive attitude. By sharing a life with a significant other, a person becomes aware that the relationship may not last forever and that it is important not to take the other person for granted. Sharing implies that both people are giving as well as taking. The power in a sharing relationship is equal, because both people are investing themselves in the relationship. Therefore, sharing is a much healthier attitude and fosters a healthy relationship.

Healthy relationships are a complex process, an ongoing, even exchange of trust, time, commitment, intimacy and caring. These are not things you see, but rather emotions and behaviors indicative of caring and love. To give these parts of oneself to another person requires a comfort with and knowledge of oneself. To attempt to give them to others without first comfortably giving these to oneself is a form of masochism. Doing so would deprive oneself of dignity and respect. One must first understand, care for, respect and love oneself before being capable of caring for, respecting or loving another person.

Eric Fromm, a well-known psychoanalyst whose work contributed to the development of the existential approach in psychology, illustrates this point extremely well. Fromm believes that human beings are constantly aware of and struggling to overcome feelings of isolation, aloneness and separateness and that often people choose to enter into relationships as a way to cope with these feelings. However, it is not possible to overcome these feelings once and for all, and a relationship will not take these feelings away. As a way to cope with these feelings, Fromm declares that we should strive for what he calls *relatedness* (some way to relate with others) and for *identity* (at-oneness, an identity that separates one from others) before entering into a relationship.

Indeed, before a person is capable of loving another person, the individual must first love him- or herself. To do this you must apply the elements of love to yourself. This basically means becoming aware of who you are—that is, your identity—and being responsible for, respecting and knowing yourself. It makes sense that you can never give to others what you have not yet given to yourself. Any attempt to do so results in empty forms of intimacy and, therefore, an unhealthy relationship.

In an attempt to seek relief from the feelings of isolation and separateness, a relationship often seems the quickest route. However, if you do not yet love yourself, then you are not capable of loving another.

Fromm identifies four alternatives for meeting one's needs when one has not learned to love oneself. The first of these, the *orgiastic state*, is extremely pertinent to our discussion of relationship violence. An orgiastic state is a temporary state of elation, similar to a state of self-induced trance. An orgiastic state may be the quickest way to gain temporary relief from the feelings of loneliness, isolation and separateness. According to Fromm, all orgiastic states have three shared characteristics:

1. They are intense, even violent at times;
2. They occur in the total personality;
3. They are transitory and periodical.

Examples of orgiastic states include having sexual orgasm, using drugs or alcohol and violence.

Sex provides a relief from the buildup of anxiety and tension. Sexual intimacy and orgasm can also create a false sense of closeness, belonging and love. However, the intensity of these sudden feelings and tension release soon lead back to guilt, shame and an increasing sense of isolation. This is due to the lack of solid spiritual relationship: two strangers shared intimate acts together, but spiritually remain empty because they do not yet love themselves and did not take the time to build a solid relationship.

The high or quick fix of sexual orgasm is much like that afforded by alcohol and drugs. Alcohol and drugs offer a quick escape by altering one's sense of perception or reality. While high or intoxicated, a person may be able to forget his or her troubles for a short time, until the person detoxifies. Afterward, however, the person has the same worries and loneliness as before, but with greater intensity, in addition to guilt and shame for taking the easy way out. There is also a great danger of becoming addicted and dependent on chemicals.

When orgiastic states are used for transitory satisfaction they often become an accepted routine and the more they occur, the greater the amount of sex, drugs or alcohol required to get the same effects. At first it may take one or two drinks to become intoxicated or one orgasm to help one forget one's troubles and feel relaxed. But over time it takes an increased amount of alcohol and/or drugs and more orgasms to achieve the same sense of pleasure, much in the same way that abuse increases in intensity over time.

When abuse is occurring it is easy to understand how violence can increase with each failed attempt at solving the problem by using an orgiastic state. Violence itself is an orgiastic state. The more feelings of isolation and frustration an abuser experiences, the more violence he may choose to use against others. Violence results in an adrenaline rush, which intensifies the effect for the abuser. The adrenaline reinforces the use of violence.

Soon the orgasms, intoxication and violence are not enough to satisfy the abuser's quest for tension relief. Force becomes more common as a means to release tension and increase the denigration and humiliation of the victim. As the abuser uses drugs and alcohol to cope, she soon finds an easy excuse for the violence—blaming it on the drug or alcohol. However, as you now realize, drugs and alcohol never make a person behave violently; violence is always a choice.

Refer to the work of Erich Fromm for more information on how we meet our needs.

CHAPTER 11

Factors of Healthy Relationships

Carl Rogers, founder of Person Centered Therapy, holds a view of the therapeutic relationship that is akin to the makeup of a healthy relationship. Although his theory is meant to pertain to the therapeutic process, I believe it also sheds light on the factors that help make fulfilling personal partnerships. He believed that therapeutic techniques are not as important or effective as the therapeutic relationship established between therapist and client. This means that the therapist's techniques will only be as effective as the therapeutic relationship is strong.

Rogers believed that the most important aspects of any therapeutic relationship are *congruence, positive regard, unconditional positive regard* and *empathy*. I believe that these are equally important in any personal relationship we enter.

Congruence refers to being genuine at any given moment, allowing oneself to express the real person. If a person were angry but smiling, her facial expression would not express her true feelings of anger. Being genuine with emotions and wants requires great risk, because an individual may be rejected by a significant other or taken advantage of, even laughed at. However, the only way to be truly genuine is to take the risk of being who you are.

Positive regard is treating a significant other in a warm, accepting, positive manner, being supporting and affirming to the significant other. A person enters a relationship to feel needed, wanted and loved. Positive regard involves letting the significant other be aware of the degree to which one respects, loves and wants the other.

Unconditional positive regard refers to the ongoing positive feeling a person has toward the significant other without any restrictions. It is unreserved, without any evaluations or limitations. Unconditional positive regard decreases the chance of experiencing disappointment because a person warmly accepts the genuine being of a significant other. It means, "I love you even when you make mistakes or let me down." It involves expecting honesty, not specific things or feelings.

Empathy refers to understanding a significant other's world as accurately as possible. This involves commitment of both time and energy. Listening is the most important skill required to hear the true message given by the significant other. It does not mean that an individual will agree with or even fully understand the partner's messages, but that one should take the time to listen and ask for clarification when needed. Empathy also involves the ability and willingness to put oneself in the other person's shoes, appreciating what the other is going through and feeling what he is feeling.

Three characteristics are essential to demonstrating genuine empathy. These are cognitive recognition, emotional connection and behavioral demonstration.

Cognitive recognition requires understanding the definition and concept of empathy. An abuser demonstrates cognitive recognition by intellectually grasping and being able to verbalize the concept of abuse and the fact that the abusive behavior has caused harm to the victim. Another feature of cognitive recognition involves understanding the concept of being a victim and appreciating what victims of abuse experience.

Emotional connection refers to experiencing and being able to identify feelings of guilt, shame and fear for the pain one's behavior has caused the victim. In addition to understanding his own behavior, an abuser must accept that he was not out of control, but rather made choices to behave abusively. The abuser must further realize that doing so means that he either did not care about the welfare or safety of the victim or truly intended to physically, psychologically and/or sexually harm the victim. Emotional connection also requires an understanding of the possible consequences of abusive behavior, such as losing a relationship or marriage; damaging relationships with the children; and the loss of love, respect and concern.

Behavioral demonstration means practicing what you preach. The abuser must do what she says she will do and behave in ways that live up to and demonstrate her beliefs, morals and values. To believe that a certain behavior is abusive, for example, yet persist in it, actually demonstrates the belief that abuse is not wrong. In fact, abusive behavior demonstrates that the abuser believes that abuse is appropriate in certain situations. If a person has true empathy, then he will not abuse his partner for any reason.

Behaviors Indicative of Empathy
Tips for Abusers

If you are not used to practicing empathy, it may be difficult to know how to begin. Use the following five behaviors as a starting point.

1. *Allow the victim to vent.* When abuse has occurred, regardless of the frequency or intensity, the victim has a right and a need to vent. He needs to talk about the abuse openly and in detail with family, friends and other supportive people. When possible he should also discuss the abuse with the abuser. This allows the victim to express his experience to the person responsible for the abuse. No resolution or marital reconciliation is possible without this healing endeavor.

2. *Discuss what the victim wants to discuss openly, patiently and respectfully.* Victims heal at their own rates: some take weeks, others years. There is no right or wrong amount of time allowed for healing. In fact, most victims will continue to

engage in the healing process throughout most of their lives. This is because victims never forget the abuse they suffered. At different times in their lives they experience situations in which they are reminded of the past abuse. When this happens, they need to resolve feelings about the past in terms of emotions evoked by the current situation. True empathy requires the abuser to realize that while the abuse occurred on the abuser's terms, the healing occurs on the victim's terms. The victim will typically remind the abuser of how her current behavior is similar to past behavior. Abusers often become frustrated with victims reminding them of past abuse, but it is important for abusers to be open to the possibility that such similarities do exist.

3. *Employ appropriate coping and problem-solving skills.* When the abuser is empathetic, he chooses to utilize healthy coping skills to address stress, anger and frustration. This means keeping calm, taking deep breaths, sticking to the current situation, demonstrating patience towards the victim and actively, openly listening.

4. *Utilize "time-outs."* When an abuser is serious about demonstrating empathy, she learns to back off for a time when escalating. Calming down and preparing for a respectful conversation sometimes require a time-out.

5. *Accept and acknowledge abusive and insensitive behavior and comments.* No person is perfect. At times, anyone can choose to be insensitive or verbally abusive. What separates the abuser from someone who engages in occasional insensitive behavior is that the nonabuser is willing to admit his behavior, takes full responsibility for it and chooses not to repeat it. The abuser, however, blames the victim, makes excuses, rationalizes and chooses to repeat the behavior.

Healthy relationships are characterized by the presence of several shared factors. It is important to realize that these factors occur with different intensities and the intensity of each may change over time and with different circumstances. The seventeen factors that help characterize a healthy relationship are

1. Trust
2. Honesty
3. Openness
4. Communication
5. Understanding
6. Flexibility/Compromise
7. Boundaries
8. Growth
9. Acceptance
10. Respect
11. Intimacy/Spirituality
12. Commitment
13. Space
14. Individuality
15 Affirmations
16. Equality
17. Risks

Each of these factors is necessary. Together they characterize a healthy relationship.

Trust

Trust is an important requirement for any relationship. It involves having confidence in and respect for your significant other as well as in yourself. Believing that your significant other is faithful first requires confidence in yourself. You must trust that you will be honest and that you will take the risk of being hurt as well as the risk of achieving a healthy relationship.

In most instances in which jealousy occurs, the significant other has done nothing to deserve such scrutiny. Jealousy indicates two things: the jealous person believes that he owns the significant other, and the jealous person is afraid of acting in the way he blames the significant other for acting. This is a matter of projection: if you're falsely accused of being unfaithful, it is likely that your significant other is struggling with his or her own issues of faithfulness. Again, one must first trust oneself; then one can trust one's significant other.

Honesty

Honesty, being genuine, involves a willingness to see oneself and a significant other as each person is, without selectivity. This means that both people are truthful about their needs, wants and beliefs and that both attempt to communicate these as directly as possible. If one partner is disappointed, he should say so. To do otherwise would only deny an emotion that exists, discrediting that person's true feelings. Spontaneity is also part of honesty and refers to reacting to or sharing the moment without planning. Honesty involves much risk.

Before you can honestly see your significant other as the person he or she truly is, you must be able to look in the mirror and see the person you really are, not just the person you want to be. Be as honest as possible about your negative and positive qualities.

Openness

Openness refers to the willingness of both partners to hear and consider each other's messages regardless of whether they believe in or agree with what is being communicated. Openness is risk in its raw state. At times a significant other may not like what she sees in her partner, but honesty, acceptance, flexibility and love all require openness.

Communication

Communication refers to the skill of receiving and giving messages and may be verbal or non-verbal. Examples of non-verbal communication include facial expressions, body posture, physical proximity and participation level. If a significant other is not returning the physical intimacy his partner desires, the non-verbal message is clear: he does not want to be doing whatever it is the partner is doing. Verbal communication is stating wants and needs and includes actually saying "yes" or "no." It is important to respect disagreements as a healthy part of any relationship. After all, there are three identities involved in any relationship.

Many people become frustrated with silence, mostly due to their own lack of a sense of security. But silences, like behaviors, often speak louder than words. If a spiritual relationship has been established, silences may bring comfort, security, a sense of belonging and union. If you or your significant other notice communication problems, then take the time to discuss the way you both communicate verbally and non-verbally. It may be in your best interest to take a class on better communication or get into couples therapy to improve communication skills.

Communication requires expressing oneself and hearing the messages one's significant other is giving. All too often we only pay attention to the messages that help us to achieve our wants. But true communication must be genuine, open and accepting to permit a relationship to grow.

Understanding

Understanding a partner takes time and a genuine willingness to truly hear what he has to say, including both verbal and nonverbal messages. It involves knowledge of both yourself and your significant other.

Understanding takes patience. However, if you continue not understanding what the other person is saying, you may begin to feel frustrated. Without an understanding of your significant other's messages, you lack understanding of his or her true feelings, wants, needs and emotions. The bottom line here is to ask about what you don't understand. When unclear about a message, ask for clarification. Although at times this may seem embarrassing, enduring the minor embarrassment could lead to an improved understanding of your significant other's message.

Flexibility

Flexibility refers to the ability to bend and compromise even when you disagree with what is being asked. Flexibility implies that there may not be a perfect answer for every situation. At times, a person simply chooses the option that makes the most sense at that moment. Even if you believe you are right and your significant other is wrong, compromising may indicate that you care about yourself, your significant other and the relationship.

It is important to remember that you do not need to give up your morals and values. Give in only to the degree that you are comfortable with or you may experience resentment and frustration as a consequence.

Boundaries

Boundaries are a vital aspect of any relationship. They mark where one person or identity ends and where the other begins. Remember that a healthy relationship involves a triad; there are three sets of boundaries to which attention must be paid. Boundaries need to be clearly identified to be effective. Without boundaries, confusion occurs.

An example of boundary confusion is if you are dependent on your significant other to the extent of doing whatever is asked of you, even when you morally disagree with it, even to the extent of giving up your own goals, rights and dreams. You become an extension of your significant other and lose much if not all of your own sense of identity. Also, the relationship will not grow when healthy boundaries do not exist, when two people are intertwined to the point of losing their own identities (see Figure 12). The result of this occurrence is a single identity instead of two crucial identities that originally made up the foundation of the relationship. It is impossible for the relationship to do anything but stagnate or decline at this point.

Growth

Remember that a healthy relationship is ever changing. Growth involves work, commitment, flexibility and responsibility. When the relationship is healthy, each of its three aspects has the chance to grow.

Growth is a healthy process even when it leads to the terminating of the relationship. As each person continues to grow, he or she may find that the relationship is not where he or she wants or needs it to be. If a person ends a relationship, it doesn't imply that either partner does not care for or love the other, but rather that one is being honest about his feelings and may have grown apart. You can truly love someone, yet not be involved in an intimate relation with that person. If you are fortunate, you may be able to maintain a friendship. However, at times, a total termination of contact occurs. The point is best summarized by the saying, "If you love something, set it free. If it comes back, it is yours. If it does not come back, it was not yours in the first place." Despite this, you may feel sad, depressed or even angry that the relationship has ended.

Respect

Respect means holding a high opinion of your significant other as an individual. It is important in any relationship and includes acceptance, healthy communication and risk taking. Respect entails making time to truly hear what your significant other is saying, even when you do not like what you hear. It requires allowing your significant other to be who he or she is and supporting the individual as he or she continues to grow and develop into who or what that person wants to become, allowing for the growth or termination of a relationship.

If you respect another person, you resist temptation to take advantage of him or her. For example, if he or she is depressed, the person may very much appreciate a hug, being held and even cuddled. But your significant other may not wish to have sex or to kiss. Respect means honoring and appreciating your significant other's emotional, physical, sexual and spiritual well-being.

Respect for others requires a comfort level with yourself, your capabilities and your limitations. You must be able to confront your own fears, hopes, dreams and reality.

Respect is a key ingredient to love and to trust. Without respect, love cannot exist. Respect of all three parts of the relationship triad is essential.

Acceptance

Acceptance involves acknowledging reality as it is and coping with it or, if dissatisfied with reality, making the necessary changes. Acceptance of oneself means allowing for strength and weakness. It is also important to accept your significant other as he or she is. Just as you allow yourself to have strengths and weaknesses, it is imperative that you allow your significant other to have strengths and weaknesses.

Acceptance also includes coming to a mutual agreement as to where the relationship is going, whether it is terminating or growing. Acceptance of termination is important. If the relationship needs to end, it is important to accept the termination so that you may move on. Doing so may increase the chance that you may continue to respect yourself and your significant other even after the termination has occurred.

Intimacy/Spirituality

Intimacy and spirituality refer to a non-verbal union—the warm feelings that being with your significant other brings, the feeling of security whether together or apart. It is experiencing belonging with another person, a sense of knowledge and deep emotion. It is somehow knowing what to say, how to touch or what to do or not to do. Intimacy allows you to bring out the best in your significant other even when the person may outshine you.

Intimacy may be social, emotional, sexual, physical and spiritual. Understanding, openness, fondness, affection, love and tenderness are aspects of intimacy.

Commitment

Commitment refers to an active investment of yourself given freely to your significant other. The investment requires giving of yourself, your time and your energy and taking risks. It is an active choice because you must decide whether or not to share yourself with another; it does not just happen. Commitment also includes an acceptance of a long-term relationship, including both the good and the bad times.

Commitment requires acceptance, trust, openness and intimacy/spirituality. Commitment—not only to each other, but to the relationship as well—involves the dedication to stand by each other through the good and bad times, to meet the needs and requests of your significant other without complaining and without compromising your values.

Space

Although a relationship involves two individuals who choose to share their lives together to form one relationship, it is imperative that the individual identities of both be allowed to grow. To expect that your significant other will always want to spend time with you, that the person will drop whatever he or she is doing upon request, is selfish. Space refers to time apart, away from your significant other. Space is healthy and when intimacy, spirituality, trust, acceptance and love are present, space brings security, not fear.

Space includes having friends, both male and female, with whom either partner can spend time. Having different interests, hobbies and activities without a dating partner is also healthy. If all of one's time is spent with a significant other, then it is likely that the relationship will become smothering and unhealthy.

Individuality

Individuality makes you different and separate from everyone else; it is the essence of who we each are. Inherent in individuality are personal traits, habits and the ability to have a separate identity from a significant other. Individuality means having your own set of male and female friends with whom you can spend time. It may also include self-sufficiency. Individuality requires boundaries. It also includes the right to set personal goals and limitations. Without individuality, relationships stagnate.

Affirmation

Affirmation refers to the process of validating the significant other as a whole person, even when one dislikes certain qualities or behaviors. This means being appreciative of a person's physical qualities and of who the person is, as well as acknowledging accomplishments. This can involve positive comments such as "You look nice," "You did a good job," or "You really mean a lot to me." It means making your partner aware of the respect and pride you have for the person and helping the person grow as an individual. Giving yourself affirmation is also important.

Equality

Equality refers to maintaining a power balance that allows both people to be the best they can be while maintaining the respect and well-being of each. Equality means not scolding the significant other when he or she displeases you, but rather accepting the fact that both people are equal, that both have strengths as well as weaknesses and that these strengths and weaknesses can be compatible. In a healthy relationship each person's strengths and weaknesses complement those of the other. Equality means that both people share power in making decisions and plans; no one person has more power than the other.

Risk

Risk involves revealing vulnerabilities, allowing oneself to be boldly right as well as boldly wrong and sharing dreams, hopes, aspiration, failures and successes with the significant other without any guarantee as to how the person will respond.

Risk means investing in the relationship without any guarantees, without ever knowing what the future will hold. Risk is an active process of being open, genuine, honest and vulnerable. Risk allows us to laugh with, not at, our significant other's strengths, weaknesses, shortcomings and dreams as well as laughing with and accepting our own.

There are no magical potions or tricks to having a healthy relationship. Healthy relationships also do not occur by chance; they require a lot of work. The work is often not difficult, but even when it is difficult, the rewards of building a healthy relationship far outweigh the effort given and sacrifices made. I believe that some factors, however, are core characteristics and that these take an extra effort to establish. The core factors include respect, trust, boundaries, growth, commitment and love. All of the other factors are in some way connected to these six.

Unhealthy relationships are characterized by the lack of these characteristics or the presence of their opposites. If any type of abuse is occurring, the relationship is unhealthy.

Factors in a Healthy Relationship	Factors in an Unhealthy Relationship
Trust	Lack of trust; jealousy may be present
Honesty, spontaneity	Deception of the significant other and self; denial of parts of reality that the abuser does not want to acknowledge
Openness	Unwillingness to share thoughts, wants and emotions; extreme privacy
Open communication	Closed, one-sided, unclear messages
Understanding	Lack of effort to become aware of the significant other's needs, feelings, wants.

Factors in a Healthy Relationship	Factors in an Unhealthy Relationship
Flexibility/compromise	Rigidity; compromise occurs only when abuser's demands are met or during honeymoon phase.
Clear boundaries	Unclear, diffuse boundaries, as if both partners are one; victim sacrifices all identity and individuality.
Growth	Stagnation; intimacy becomes a routine chore.
Acceptance of self, partner and relationship	Little or no acceptance of self, partner or relationship
Respect	Belief that one partner is godlike while the other is worthless; respect demanded by abuser, but none given in return.
Intimacy/spirituality	No warm feelings; intimacy is like a chore; fear is present; force may be used.
Commitment is an active choice.	Both partners are committed only to one person's needs; victim feels trapped.
Space	Victim expected to spend all free time with abuser; may give up friends, family, school, job; victim feels isolated.
Individuality	Differences not respected and growth not fostered.

Factors in a Healthy Relationship	Factors in an Unhealthy Relationship
Affirmations	Affirmation only when victim gives in to demands or during honeymoon phase.
Equality, shared power	A one-up, one-down situation; force and coercion are used. Physical, psychological and sexual violence may occur.
Risks taken by both partners.	Avoidance of risks by victim; victim afraid to express emotions, wants or needs for fear of further abuse.

Each of these seventeen factors may occur with its own intensity. Over time certain factors may be present more than others. It is also important to be aware that some healthy factors may be present even in an unhealthy, abusive relationship. Maintaining a good relationship requires an ongoing evaluation of how each person's needs are being met, as well as an effort to ensure that all seventeen factors are present.

Healthy relationships take time to develop. That is where commitment comes in—a commitment not only to energy and effort but to the significant other as well. Although some people believe that love and the development of a healthy relationship may occur instantaneously, they are only fooling themselves into settling for a relationship that will not produce the strong positive feelings they are hoping for, and such a fast occurring relationship will probably not be long-lasting. Love requires patience, time, perseverance and a willingness to take many risks.

CHAPTER 12

Understanding and Helping Victims

Why Victims Remain in Abusive Relationships

Victims of abuse often remain in abusive relationships and this raises serious questions. Why would someone remain in a relationship with a person who is verbally or physically abusive, controlling, mean and self-centered? Why not simply leave? Why not find a nonabusive partner? Numerous factors sway victims to remain in abusive relationships. Many are not difficult to understand.

Fear is perhaps the most influential of these factors. Of utmost concern is physical safety. Having experienced a multitude of abuses ranging from seemingly mild verbal abuse to physical assault and even rape, the victim has learned that the abuser is in control and that the abuser lacks any significant care about the victim's well-being.

The victim may also fear for his relationship with the children. In addition to the threat of losing custody of the children, victims must worry about having their children brainwashed against them. Abusers are very skilled at influencing children with strategies that range from threats to spoiling them in order to buy their loyalty.

Most victims also fear not being believed. Abusers lie to victims' family members and friends and—at least initially—abuse only when others cannot witness their actions. An abuser also may portray the victim as being emotionally unstable, unreasonable and the primary abuser. Often when the police are called, the abuser appears calm, caring and cooperative, having already vented her anger. Many law enforcement personnel, family members and friends fail to understand this dynamic, so the victim's fear of not being believed is justified. If others have discounted the victim's story in the past, he has all the more reason to expect that others will not believe him.

The more likeable and active the abuser is with the victim's family and social network, the more difficult it is for the victim to leave. If the abuser is well known and liked in the community, the victim's allegations may seem less believable to others. The abuser's role within the family and social support network is even more powerful if the victim has a history of prior abuse or depression, lacks a stable employment history or appears more fragile and vulnerable than the abuser. Others may view the victim's claims of abuse as being vindictive. If the victim's support system in any way condones the abuse or sides with the abuser, the victim is psychologically pressured to stay with the abuser. At some point, the victim may become so depressed and hopeless that she will give up and decide to remain in the abusive relationship.

Abuse results in a diminished ability for the victim to trust others. Many victims experience difficulty trusting that others will believe them or help them. They may fear that others will take advantage of their weakness and vulnerability. Despite the abuse, the abuser is at least somewhat predictable; the victim can be confident that the abuser will demonstrate some caring and loving behavior during the honeymoon phase before returning to abusive behavior.

An abuser may employ other tactics to isolate the victim. He may use lies, harassment and, at times, threats to drive a wedge between the victim and the support network. The victim's friends and family may also spend less and less time with her because they see the abuse but feel unable to help. This sense of frustration on the part of the victim's support network increases the victim's sense of frustration, strain, embarrassment and helplessness. Victims of abuse experience great confusion about what to do and who to tell. Lacking an effective support system makes it that much more difficult for a victim to get out of an abusive relationship.

Over time, a victim may begin to view her life and relationship in a delusional manner. She may experience a sense that her reaction to the abuse must indicate that she is insane. Abusers are masters of disguise, often appearing to be two distinct people, at one moment being loving and caring and the next controlling, conniving and abusive. During the honeymoon stage, the victim often begins to doubt whether her partner is abusive and to experience difficulty reconciling how the abuser can shift from loving to mean in a matter of minutes with little or no warning.

Many victims do not leave abusive relationships because they believe that they deserve to be abused or are somehow to blame. Time and time again I hear from victims statements such as, "I asked for it," "I should have backed down and I didn't," "I have abused him as well," and "It really wasn't that bad; I deserved it." Victims often have low self-esteem even if they are highly educated, independent and outgoing people. Over time, abusers successfully chip away at and attack victims' strength, self-worth and values. The abuser breaks the victim down, making the victim increasingly vulnerable and dependent until she begins to accept that she must in some way deserve to be mistreated. As they come to experience low self-esteem, victims begin to believe that they have no ability to impact the abuser or to leave the relationship. Victims remain in the relationships because they feel powerless and hopeless.

Choosing to stay may make the victims feel responsible for the abuse. This feeling is accurate to a certain extent: if the victim chose to leave the relationship, the abuser could not abuse her in the same manner or might not be able to abuse her at all. The important thing to remember, though, is that the abuser makes a conscious decision to abuse, regardless of what the victim does or does not do. The victim can be empowered with the knowledge that if he leaves the relationship, the abuse will likely end; however, remaining in the relationship in no way makes the victim responsible for the abuser's choice to abuse.

Victims often experience a sense of embarrassment not only for having been abused, but for their partners' abusive behavior. This sense of embarrassment may prevent them from seeking help.

A victim may remain in an abusive relationship because of the mistaken belief that she can change the abuser. Many people want to help others by trying to change them. Parents want to change their children. Lovers want to change their partners' negative or irritating behaviors. Victims want to help their partners to cease the abusive behavior. The problem is that if the abuser does not really want to change, all the help in the world will make no difference. I have found through my work that approximately 80 percent of abusers will fail to cease their abusive behavior. Society can penalize, fine, incarcerate and, in some states, even assign the death penalty for certain crimes, but we have not yet found a successful way to force people to change.

A victim's other beliefs may convince him to remain in an abusive relationship. Some people feel that having a lover or spouse is necessary. Society encourages relationships. Most people want to be in a long-term, committed relationship; when they are not, they may feel unattractive, unwanted or unlovable. Victims do not want to be alone and may go to extremes of protecting abusers to avoid the loss of relationships.

In a similar fashion, many victims believe that they must tolerate abuse because of commitments they have made. Marital vows often appear to force husband and wife to remain in the marriage and may result in the victim feeling trapped. "For better or for worse" was never meant to include being abused, used, lied to or cheated on, but ending a relationship or marriage may not seem like a viable option to the victim if her beliefs discourage divorce.

It was not that long ago that our society viewed jealousy as a sign of love. Although we have since redefined jealousy as a form of control, harassment and abuse, many victims have been brainwashed to believe that it is an indication of affection. Strict religious circles and cults sometimes reinforce these myths. Many abusers tell their victims, "I only get jealous because I love you." The more isolated the victim, the more likely he becomes to accept the abuse, control and jealousy as normal parts of a relationship.

Many victims deny and minimize the extent of the abuse. This occurs as the psyche, or ego, tries to protect the victim from the pain of full awareness of the seriousness of the abuse. Some victims will report the abuser to others, including law enforcement, only to recant their statements at a later time. This is not a sign of deceitfulness, but rather an indication that the abuse has become so emotionally severe that the victim fears for her very survival. When the victim withdraws statements or minimizes what has occurred, the abuse is likely severe and may result in serious physical harm or even murder.

Most victims are unaware of where to obtain help. Many have at best vague understandings of who offers services and what those services involve. This may result in the victim accepting the abuse and remaining in the relationship because he sees no way out.

Similarly, most are unaware of their legal rights. Abusers repeatedly tell their victims
- That they will take the children away
- That the victim will have no financial support
- That the victim will have no social support
- That they will portray the victim as unfit or unfaithful or make other derogatory statements.

Without knowledge of her legal rights, a victim may feel that it would be impossible for her to escape the abuser.

How to Help a Victim

The many factors pressuring victims to remain in abusive relationships make encouragement and support from others that much more important. If someone you care about is struggling with abuse, you can help him or her decide to report the abuse and leave the relationship temporarily or permanently. Begin with the following steps:

1. Help the victim to understand that every decision he or she makes is a powerful statement. Make it clear that even inaction sends a message to the abuser that abuse is acceptable and will be tolerated.

2. Explain to the victim that standing up to the abuser by reporting the abuse to the police and to others is the first step in protecting him- or herself.

3. If the victim has children, help him or her to recognize his or her obligation to protect them. A victim who is unable to protect him- or herself from the abuser is not capable of protecting the children. The victim must come to believe that failure to take action places his children in the abuser's path of violence.

4. Make the victim aware of his or her rights and the resources available to him or her. He or she must be informed about how to obtain professional support.

5. Educate the victim about economic matters. Often the abuser has forced the victim to believe that he or she will be without financial support if he or she leaves. Find out how local laws can help the victim obtain financial assistance. Also investigate the victim's options for employment and education.

6. Help the victim arrange to receive therapeutic services from a qualified professional. Find someone specializing in working with abuse victims.

7. Assist the victim in accessing any necessary services. This can be as simple as driving him or her to an appointment.

8. Ensure that the victim receives required services promptly. Professionals should make time within twenty-four hours of a victim's request for help. Any delay may encourage the victim to minimize the seriousness of the situation and increase the likelihood that he or she will remain in the abusive relationship.

9. Help the victim to learn about separation, divorce and how to obtain an attorney.

10. Ensure that the victim has accurate information about psychological and verbal, physical and sexual abuse.

11. Help the victim to obtain a restraining order or order for protection. Encourage the victim to report any violation of such orders. Victims need others to assertively protect them from abusers.

12. Help the victim avoid any contact with the abuser. Many abusers disobey no contact orders. Family, friends, coworkers, neighbors and everyone involved in the victim's life should help the victim be safe.

13. Find out what policies the victim's employer or school has to prevent harassment, violence and abuse from occurring and make sure that these are enforced. Since there is no effective way to avoid contact between the abuser and victim if they attend the same school, educational professionals need to ensure that the abuser is no longer on campus. Part of the consequences to the abuser should be expulsion, regardless of whether the abuse occurred on school grounds or at a school activity. Schools and employers have a legal and ethical obligation to protect students and employees. Enormous lawsuits have been settled in favor of the victim when agencies have failed to protect the victim from the abuser.

14. Listen. Encourage the victim to share his or her story. The best medicine is telling others, breaking the silence and getting the support necessary to heal.

15. Believe the victim and let him or her know that you do. As I explained earlier, fear that others will not believe them often keeps victims in abusive relationships; you can help allay this fear. While it is true the victims may at times exaggerate the extent of the abuse, most of what they report will be accurate.

16. Respect the victim. Having been through attacks on his or her entire identity and assaults on his or her body, he or she now needs and deserves to be treated as a human being with value, regardless of his or her flaws.

17. Never blame the victim for the abuse. Realize that the victim may have

- Had an ongoing relationship with the abuser
- Had several sexual partners or a reputation of being promiscuous
- Used drugs and/or alcohol at the time of the abuse or sexual assault
- Dressed provocatively or in revealing clothing
- Behaved flirtatiously
- Been naïve and overly trusting
- Given permission to be sexual with the abuser but changed his or her mind
- Agreed to other sexual behavior than what the abuser forced
- Put him- or herself in a risky situation
- Not resisted
- Allowed the abuser to make contact or disregard a no contact order, order for protection or restraining order.

Regardless of what the victim did or failed to do, only the abuser can be held accountable for the choice to be abusive. Sex offenders and abusers do not care about how a victim dresses or behaves; their crimes are about gaining power and control over victims. A victim may already be contending with professionals who question the situation, because the victim's behavior appears to offer the abuser an alibi. Remember that nothing the victim did ever makes him or her responsible for the abuse. Be sure the victim knows this as well.

18. Understand that inconsistencies in facts occur naturally from victims of psychological, physical and sexual abuse. It is common for victims to recall different details at different times. It is also common for victims to recant allegations of abuse, usually out of a sense of undue guilt and pressure from abusers or others. The original statements are almost always the most factual when investigated.

19. Teach the victim that fear is kept alive by inaction. The fear will subside as he or she asks for and accepts help from others and as he or she tells his or her story of abuse.

CHAPTER 13

Sexual Behavior and Abuse

Just as relationships may be healthy or unhealthy, sexual behavior may also be healthy or unhealthy. All of the factors that help make relationships healthy (see Chapter 11) also apply to healthy sexual contact. The most important factor, however, is respect. Without respect there can never be love. Healthy sexual behavior demands respect and love. Respect is the factor that most differentiates unhealthy sexual behavior from healthy sexual behavior.

Often people become involved sexually with a significant other before an attempt is made to build a genuine, solid relationship. Solid relationships take time to develop. Although sex may create an illusion of love, all that may exist without a solid relationship is temporary relief from loneliness.

Most people take sexual contact for granted, simply expecting it as a result of dating someone. Most people never fully understand or appreciate the intimacy and spirituality that are an integral part of healthy sexual behavior. Intimacy is the closeness of two people that results from mutual respect, openness, a willingness to grow and, of course, love. Intimacy is spiritual; it cannot be seen or physically touched but is instead felt or experienced.

Intimacy may include sexual contact, but *sexual contact does not have to be involved.*

As a result of not attempting to establish a solid relationship that involves intimacy and spirituality, many people do not have healthy sexual contact. Many people strive only for physical pleasure or orgasm. When the goal of sexual contact is only to feel good, then the beauty of sexual intimacy is lost and intimacy and spirituality cannot occur. As a result, both people feel empty and far apart, and at least one person may feel used and victimized.

Healthy sexual contact allows both people to make their wants known and to have their wants met. This does not guarantee that one person will meet all requests of the other, but rather that both partners will at least have the opportunity to communicate their requests.

In Chapter 1, I defined sexual abuse as any forced sexual contact. Sexual assault covers several different types of sexual violence, including date rape and stranger rape. Date rape refers to a sexual assault or rape that occurs during a date or when the abuser is involved in a dating relationship with the victim. A person who commits date rape does not care for the victim. Just as all abuse is a planned, conscious choice made by the abuser, sexual assault, date rape and stranger rape are also planned acts of violence.

Sexual assault does not just happen, as some people believe. All rapes are planned. Abusers make the decision to have their demands met without regard for victims' rights or well-being. It is estimated that in 90 percent of all cases of sexual assault and rape the victim knows the rapist.

Women are not the only victims of date rape. Men can be coerced and physically forced into being sexual just as women can. Although statistics on the number of males who are date raped are difficult to come by, from my research and counseling I estimate that nearly 30 percent of all victims who experience date rape are male.

Two types of force may be used to compel people into having sex against their wills: psychological and physical. When physical force is used, physical abuse also occurs, because the abuser physically attacks the victim and forces sexual contact. Physical force may include hitting, restraining, removing the victim's clothing and performing any sexual act on the victim without consent. This may mean forcing the victim to be touched, making the victim touch the abuser's genitals or any forced penetration (Penetration is the insertion of any object or body part into any body opening; this includes oral, anal and vaginal penetration). The use of physical force as described constitutes date rape.

Many date rapes, however, do not include the use of physical force but rather the use of coercion, or psychological force. Coercion refers to the use of tricks, pressure or threats to make people perform acts against their wills. There are two types of coercion: psychological strategies and threats. Psychological strategies include *intimidation, emotional blackmail, game playing, pressuring, boundary violations* and *lying.*

Intimidation is the act of causing partners to experience fear for their safety or to doubt whether they are normal or sane. Examples include statements such as "What's wrong with you that you don't want to have sex with me?" "Everyone else is doing it, why don't you?" and "You've got me turned on, so now you have to please me." The goal of intimidation is to make the significant other feel somehow responsible and guilty for the abuser's own sexual arousal, thereby attempting to force or trick the victim into sexual contact.

> *Angie and Dave had been dating a couple of months. Dave complained that she flirted with other men whenever they went out and that she hinted that she might have sex with other men if he did not satisfy her. Dave cared very much for Angie but sometimes found himself too tired to have sex after work. Angie had trouble accepting his not wanting to have sex.*
>
> *Angie believed that men are always in the mood for having sex unless they have been cheating. So when Dave said no, she assumed that he was either having an affair or not sexually attracted to her. Angie had manipulated Dave into having sex several times. She made him feel guilty and attacked his masculine image. She would fondle him and lie on top of him while kissing. Even when Dave*

said no, she continued to seduce him until he gave in or angrily said no.

Dave was having a difficult time with his own sense of masculinity, because he also believed that men should always be ready for sex. He became depressed when he found that he did not always want to have sex with Angie. He also felt extremely sexually and emotionally attracted to her, which further confused him. In our sessions together, both learned about sexuality, dispelling sexual myths, and learned to accept that men, just like women, can say no to sex and are not always in the mood for sex. They managed to grow closer together and continued their relationship.

Emotional blackmail occurs when love and other emotions are used to coerce a dating partner into having sex. Examples include statements such as "If you loved me, you would have sex with me" and "Prove that you love me." The goal is to equate sex with love.

Game playing refers to mind games used to get a significant other to give in to sexual demands. Examples include statements such as "If you don't have sex with me, I'll find someone who will" and "I'll stop dating you if you don't." Abusers use game playing to make victims believe that they are not giving equally to the relationship and that they should be giving in to the abuser's demands.

Pressuring refers to the use of nagging, begging and whining as a way to coerce sex from a partner. Examples may include repeating demands over and over again with words to make the victim feel sorry for the abuser, such as "Come on," and "Please do this for me." These are repeated until the victim gives in to the abuser's demands.

Boundary violations occur when an abuser violates the victim's space and body. The space violations may continue even after the significant other has said "no" or "stop." Examples include removing the abuser's or the significant other's clothing, beginning to have sex without the partner's consent and refusing to let the victim leave the situation.

Lying refers to the blatant lies that are told by an abuser to get the victim to have sex. Examples include agreeing only to fondle and then going beyond the agreed-upon limits. Some abusers also make promises to their significant others to get sex, but then refuse to keep or honor the promises.

The second type of force is the use of threats. (Threats were described in Chapter 2.) Again, threats occur any time an abuser warns the victim that the abuser may use force to get sex if the partner refuses to give in to demands. Examples may include threatening to use physical violence, spread rumors, have an affair or even terminate the relationship. Threats, like psychological strategies, play on the emotions of the victim, especially the emotions of confusion and fear.

If any of the above types of coercion are used to get sexual contact, date rape has occurred. Most date rapes involve the use of coercion, not physical force. It is important to point out that coercion and physical force may be equally devastating to the victim. Abusers are aware of what they are doing—committing rape—or at least understand that they are harming and exerting force against their victims. Force does not just occur on its own; individuals have to make a conscious decision to use force. When an abuser talks a victim into doing something the victim does not want to do, this is coercion.

While it is true that a victim can always say no to sexual activity, he or she may be risking further sexual and physical harm by refusing. If given a choice between being physically forced into having sex or allowing the abuser to have sex with a victim as a result of psychological force, the victim may choose to give in and cooperate as a means to avoid further harm. But this is still date rape. The victim is not really given a choice; he or she is damned for cooperating and damned for resisting.

When a victim is coerced into sexual activity, he or she experiences fear—fear not only of experiencing further physical and sexual harm, but also of losing the person he or she cares about. I believe that most rape victims are faced with a dual crisis. The first crisis involves actual abuse, rape or attempted rape. The second crisis involves the dilemma of "hating the one you love." When the person expected to love and respect you violates not only your body but also your mind, he or she violates your whole being. The hardest, most painful part of being date-raped may be dealing with the fact that without respect, love cannot exist and therefore the abuser does not love the victim.

Victims of abuse—whether it is physical or sexual abuse—often attempt to blame themselves for the abusive act. It is common for a rape victim to blame himself rather than place the blame on the person he loves. Victims make statements such as "I should have said yes anyway." "He is under so much stress that he couldn't help it," "I got her turned on," or "I need to be less selfish and more giving of myself." Many victims believe that they were raped or physically abused as a result of something they did or did not do, or due to the way they dress or talk. But the truth is that regardless of how a person dresses, talks or behaves, no one ever deserves or asks to be raped or abused.

Abusers do not decide to rape on the basis of looks or behaviors, but rather because of the issues of power and control (discussed in Chapter 5) and the desire to humiliate and degrade the victim. Abusers who commit date rape want to force their partners to do something against the victims' wills that will result in humiliation and degradation. Rape is always a conscious choice an abuser makes and no one causes an abuser to rape someone. Rape is never the victim's fault, ever. Regardless of how much the abuser feels that he or she is being led on, teased or provoked, it is important to remember that the abuser makes a choice to commit the rape, often even before the date begins. All rapes are planned; they never just happen.

There is also no such thing as being out of control sexually, although many people use this as an excuse to get their partners to continue sexual contact. Once someone says "stop" or "no" or refuses to participate, it is rape if sexual contact continues. "I don't know," "Maybe," "Not now," "Later," "I'm scared," "Please don't" and "Wait" all should be considered synonymous with "no." When a person refuses to give permission to engage in sexual behavior and the other person engages in sexual contact, rape is occurring.

Rape is not an act of sexual intimacy, but rather one of power, control and degradation. It appears much easier to believe this when referring to a stranger rape versus a date rape. When the rape occurs between acquaintances or significant others, it somehow seems less criminal and less important. Yet no matter how it is termed, forced or coerced sex is rape and there is no justification. Rape is a crime of violence in which sex is used as the weapon. Acts of passion may include kissing, hugging and other intimate types of behavior, but the key ingredient that differentiates passion from rape is respect. Abusers do not listen to or respect victims' requests and well-being.

One unfortunate way many victims cope with date rape is to block out the experience. Afterward many victims talk of the occurrence as if they were watching someone else, not themselves, being raped. This is called disassociation and is a way to mentally escape the pain of being physically and sexually assaulted. While it is effective for blocking out the bad experience in the short run, in the long run it can lead to many problems that may take years to resolve.

Healthy sexual behavior always allows both individuals to have power in deciding what type of sexual contact will occur. If people truly respect and love their significant others, they listen to and honor their decision when they say no to sexual contact. Healthy sexual behaviors involve three crucial factors: *consent, respect* and *intimacy and spirituality*. The intimacy and spirituality involved in healthy sexual behaviors are the same as those in healthy relationships (see Chapter 11), but consent and respect merit further explanation.

Consent

Consent refers to giving permission and agreeing on what will happen. In order for consent to be given

- The other person must have the right and safety to say yes or no without being forced. This means that the person is not being threatened in any way.

- The person must fully understand what she is agreeing to do. It is important that both people speak the same language at least somewhat fluently and are both able to communicate their understanding.
- The person must be in a clear state of mind, that is, not impaired in any way. Impairment would include being under the influence of drugs or alcohol, mentally ill, asleep or injured. If somebody has to be under the influence of drugs or alcohol before he will consent to sexual activity, he does not want to have sex. If a person is in any state of physical or mental impairment, she is not in a state legally to give consent.

After consent has been given, the next step is to set the sexual boundary—that is, to decide and agree on what type of sexual contact will occur. It is important to set sexual boundaries in advance when possible. Waiting until the last moment to ask for consent may result in frustration and disappointment. Setting sexual boundaries allows both people to understand what each person would like to share. If you want to fondle or have foreplay but not have intercourse, say so. Agree to only what you feel comfortable doing; remember that it is your right to set sexual boundaries.

The relationship of Cindy and Bill illustrates a problem with lack of consent.

When Bill wanted to have sex with Cindy, he often made sure that she had been drinking and was intoxicated. Cindy often refused to have sex with him, because she wanted more from their relationship than just sex. Bill became angry when she refused him and accused her of having sexual affairs with men she knew. Sometimes Bill became sad and told her that he really needed to have sex with her to help him feel better. Sometimes Cindy gave in to his demands and manipulation.

When Cindy had been drinking, she was not able to physically resist Bill as well as when she was sober. She found it more difficult to push him away and if she wanted to leave, Bill would refuse to drive her home, leaving her stranded and vulnerable. Bill frequently used guilt to make Cindy feel as if she was not giving as much to their relationship as she should have. Cindy's friends all agreed that Bill was abusive, but Cindy would not leave him.

In our sessions, Cindy began to identify that after having been manipulated into having sex with Bill she felt hurt, violated, ill and used. Bill felt in control, guilty and satisfied. Unfortunately Bill was not willing to examine his abusiveness any further. He broke up with Cindy. Cindy continued to learn more about abuse and date rape and chose to continue with therapy. The more she resolved and learned, the stronger she became and the happier she found herself. She can now set sexual boundaries without feeling raped or guilty.

Respect

Respect requires accepting a significant other's boundaries as well as one's own. Also included here is the responsibility for discussing birth control methods and sexually transmitted diseases honestly and openly. If you are close enough to have sex with your significant other, then you are close enough to take the risk of discussing these issues. It is better to experience some embarrassment before engaging in sexual contact than to deal with these issues after finding out that one person contracted a sexually transmitted disease from the other or that pregnancy occurred.

Respect means not taking advantage of a significant other's physical or emotional state and it involves watching out for the other person's well-being. If a significant other needs a hug because he or she is depressed, for example, it is probably not the time to ask for further sexual contact. Putting the other's needs before one's own and being willing to compromise is respect in action.

If you or your significant other has a change of heart and decides not to have sex, even after agreeing to or during sexual activity, it is imperative to stop! Everyone has the right to a change of mind. We all have changed our decisions concerning sexual activities at one time or another. It is a myth that men always want to have sex or that once sexual behavior has begun, it cannot stop until it is finished.

Respect is putting the needs and best interest of a significant other before one's own, without sacrificing one's own morals and values. If both people cannot agree on sexual boundaries, then it may be time to end the relationship and find others who are more compatible. There are only two types of sex: consensual and forced.

We don't want to disappoint the people we love; we strive to please them. But if the sexual contact means more to a significant other than respecting your rights, then that person does not love you. It is as simple as that. If a partner cannot accept the fact that no means no, listen to the message being given. If forced sexual contact occurs, it will be exploitative, empty sex. If your significant other physically forces you or coerces you into having sex, that is not an indication of love, passion or intimacy. It is rape, violence and abuse.

A case with which I was involved is a common one on college campuses and high school dating scenes.

Adam was a star on the football team at college. Everybody seemed to like him. He was good looking, outgoing and friendly, and many females wanted to go out with him. He maintained a 3.5 grade point average and frequented the major parties. He asked Kris out on a date and they planned to go out for pizza and then to a party.

Adam brought her flowers and they talked all the way to the restaurant. During dinner, they seemed to get along fine. Kris felt special, knowing that this well-liked man was interested in her; what a self-esteem boost! She felt that she could trust Adam and agreed to go to the party, which was at his house. There were thirty to fifty people at the party. Everybody was talking and dancing and the music was loud. Kris and Adam began to drink.

Later that night, Adam wanted to take Kris on a tour of the house. She agreed. When they got to one of the bedrooms, Adam said, "This is my room and I have something to show you on the dresser."

Kris entered the bedroom and Adam closed the door. "Kris, you're so beautiful and I really like you. I want to see you again." Kris was flattered. Adam told her to sit on the bed. He pulled her to sit down, put his arm around her and began to kiss her. The kissing was nice.

Adam then pushed her down on the bed, got on top of her and began to take their clothes off. He kissed her hard, preventing her from screaming or telling him to stop. Kris attempted to fight him, but before she could do anything, he was having intercourse with her. Adam was raping Kris. Afterward, Adam threatened Kris that if she ever told anyone he would smear her name, give her a bad reputation and physically hurt her. Then he drove her home.

Kris was scared and confused; how could a popular, well-respected man who seemed so gentle hurt her? She blamed herself. She did not tell anyone.

While Kris was attending another party with her girlfriends, Adam's friend approached her and pulled her to an upstairs bedroom. Adam was there. They turned off the lights, called Kris a slut and proceeded to gang rape her. Her screams could not be heard due to the loud music. Her friends found her wandering outside, dazed and confused. They drove her to the emergency room.

Kris was treated for rape. She received therapy for many months and had to drop out of school. It took time before Kris could label what happened to her as rape and blame Adam and his friends, not herself. Finally Kris went to the authorities. Adam was arrested and, in therapy, told of his plan to set her up to be raped.

CHAPTER 14

Rules for Healthy Problem Resolution

Problems and disagreements occur in every relationship. Every problem and argument has at least two participants. One participant's job may be to argue and the other may be expected to somehow respond. However, the problem affects both people. If problems are not dealt with promptly and directly, anger, guilt, disappointment and resentment may be not only experienced but also heightened to such a degree that the relationship begins to deteriorate.

The best solution to dealing with problems is healthy discussion. Many people choose to refer to "rules for fair fighting." However, using the term "fair fighting" somehow seems to validate violence by supporting the belief that as long as the fighting occurred during a "fair fight," it is somehow condoned. Healthy problem resolution is not fighting but discussion. It involves strict rules and no one person wins; rather, both people triumph, because when a healthy discussion occurs, the relationship is almost always strengthened. Some rules for healthy, nonviolent problem resolution follow.

Timing

Address the issue when both you and your significant other have the time, energy and willingness to engage in the discussion. Allow time not only to discuss the issues, but also to show support afterward.

Use "I" Statements

Take responsibility by owning your thoughts, feelings and behaviors. Use "I" statements and avoid "you," "us" or "we" when referring to the issue. Taking responsibility can lessen defenses and may encourage both you and your significant other to calm down and show respect and support for each other.

Give and Accept Feedback

If you are unwilling to accept feedback, don't give it! However, be aware that the only way to resolve a conflict while maintaining respect is through clear, open, two-way feedback.

Here and Now

It is important to stick to the present issue. Bringing up other issues, especially old ones, will only confuse the discussion. Specify what issue will be discussed and stick to it. If other issues arise, take a break before discussing the next issue. This will decrease confusion and allow each person to physically and mentally prepare for the next discussion.

No Attacking Your Significant Other

Avoid bringing up issues and problems that neither of you can change. You can never undo something you have done in the past; however, you can deal with current emotions resulting from past behavior. Avoid using your significant other's problems (e.g., depression, illness, childhood abuse, loss and grief) against him or her.

Respect

Respect both yourself and your significant other. This includes allowing the other person to finish what he or she wants to say without being interrupted or threatened, as well as allowing for tears, a break from the discussion and time-outs.

Hold Hands and Face Each Other at Eye Level

Discuss issues in an optimal setting that allows for good communication to occur. Avoid having the television or radio on or being somewhere where someone may interrupt your discussion. If possible, sit across from each other in chairs at a table, on a couch or on the floor. This will increase eye contact. Holding hands can add warmth while allowing for a feeling of equality, security and safety. The goal is to avoid a one-up, one-down setting.

Avoid Sarcasm

Put-downs and jokes have no place in a serious discussion. Sarcasm is not respectful and may result in a premature end of the discussion. Sarcasm may continue to build and breed resentments, placing the relationship in jeopardy.

Never Attempt to Win

Either you both win or you both lose. If your goal is to maintain the relationship, it does not really matter who is right or wrong. Focus on resolving the problem without judgment as to who is right or wrong. Even when you may be right, it is better to compromise at times than to satisfy your ego's need to show your significant other up by winning.

Express Feelings Appropriately

It is important to openly and honestly express your feelings. It is most effective to express your feelings at the time that you are experiencing them. Don't wait for days or weeks; this may result in the intensification of feelings as well as building up resentment, frustration and anger.

Compromise

No one is always right or always wrong. Your beliefs may be different from your significant other's. Remember that the goal is to maintain the relationship, not to prove who is right or wrong or to put one over the other. Maintaining a relationship requires bending even when you know you may be right. However, being flexible and compromising does not mean you have to give up your morals or values. Only give in to the point that you are morally comfortable with.

Never Assume Meanings or Intentions

If you are not sure what your significant other is saying, ask. Only through inquiry can you clearly understand what the other person is truly saying. Also, you can never know what the other is trying to say or what he or she means without that person telling you.

No Mind Games

If your goal is to remain together, don't play games. No one is less or more powerful than the other. Treat your significant other with respect. Do not prematurely apologize or refuse to take the other's concerns seriously. Falsely giving in results in increased resentment and taller, stronger walls between you. Mind games played by one person are a form of manipulation that serves to put the other person down.

Speak Only for Yourself

You are an expert on yourself while your significant other is an expert on him- or herself. Speaking for your significant other only serves to devalue his or her feelings and thoughts and teaches the other person that you believe yourself more knowledgeable about the person than he or she is.

Do Not Punish the Other

If you want to engage in an intimate adult relationship, act it. A parent-child relationship may include discipline, but a dating relationship requires equality and maturity in power. It is not one partner's job to discipline the other. If you feel the urge to punish, take a time out and refocus on what the real issue is and what your role in the issue is. Remember that every argument has at least two participants and each is responsible for the problem to some degree.

Time Out and Termination

If you need to end the discussion before it is finished, set a time to resume it. Avoiding the issue will only exacerbate the problem and increase resentment. Also, check with your significant other before ending. Attempt to end the discussion when both of you agree on ending. If you recognize that you are escalating, take a time-out, tell your significant other how long you will be gone and leave quietly. When you return, ask if the other person is ready to continue the discussion, but only if you know you are ready.

No Violence

There must be trust for issues to be resolved and violence is the quickest way to destroy any and all trust. Even if one of you has hurt the other, violence is never justified, asked for or deserved. Remember that provocation only challenges a person; it is that person who decides how to act. No one is ever out of control.

Wrap-Up and Discussion

When the discussion is finished, talk about the process. How does it feel to follow these rules? Did you feel hurt, misunderstood or respected? Regardless of whether the issue was resolved, was the discussion worth it? How was the relationship affected by the discussion? Paying attention to and discussing how the problem-solving process went will not only strengthen the relationship but increase the chance of a healthy discussion happening again.

Reward and Intimacy

At the end of the talk, reward yourself and your significant other. Give hugs, shake hands or whatever form of intimacy is appropriate at the time. This will feel good and increase the likelihood of a healthy discussion occurring again. It will also serve to show your significant other how important he or she really is to you. Even when you know you were wrong, owning what you did or said and taking responsibility for yourself feels great.

These guidelines are offered as a model for healthy problem resolution. No one is perfect, but each person can be respectful even when making a mistake. Keep a copy of these rules nearby so you can use them during a discussion. And remember that no one person wins in a relationship. Either both people win or both people lose.

Problem Solving Strategies

1. Take a deep, deep breath and hold it. Slowly let the air out. This involves getting "fat," expanding your gut and filling your lungs fully with air. Do so with your mouth open. This has the effect of a turkey dinner, relaxing you and settling you down. If you breathe through your nose or with your mouth only partially open, you are taking shallow breaths and starving your body for oxygen, which causes the "fight or flight" response. If your goal is to remain calm and resolve a problem respectfully, then you need to take a deep, deep breath. You may have to take a few to calm down.

2. Smile. When you smile, you guide your body and mind to relaxation. It is difficult to remain angry or to behave abusively when smiling.

3. Write out your response. Take time to review what it is that you want to say or do. Then decide. Sometimes deciding to say or to do nothing is appropriate.

4. Begin your comment or response with "I love you" whenever possible. This helps to ensure that your response and interaction will be respectful rather than angry, hostile or abusive. At the very least, remind yourself that you respect the other person.

CHAPTER 15

Separation
and Divorce

Marriage is often thought to somehow "cure" abusive tendencies, but this is a myth. If an abuser and a victim marry each other, the abuse will continue and will intensify as time goes by. Marriage requires much more commitment, teamwork and trust than any dating relationship. Inherently, marriage results in much more stress than a dating relationship. Ending any abusive relationship is difficult, but ending an abusive marriage is far more complex. There is property to divide, spousal support, child support, severe emotional stress, extended family division and so on. There may be additional social pressure to remain together, because marriage is considered a life-long commitment. Married couples or those living together in abusive relationships must face the possibility of separation and, in some cases, divorce.

Separation, which involves one partner moving into another residence, is almost always necessary even if the couple ultimately decides to remain together. It offers both parties space, an opportunity to think and prepare, and safety. If the abuser is the one to leave, the victim and children can work on reestablishing trust, security and sanity in the home. During the separation, the victim can get a better reading as to whether the abuser is willing to accept responsibility for his abusive behavior and whether he will cooperate with the separation and all court orders. The time alone can motivate the abuser to cease the abusive behavior. Without separation, the abuser is highly likely to continue to engage in verbally and psychologically abusive behavior, even while in treatment. The relationship almost always ends if the couple does not take time apart.

Abusers who are unwilling to accept full responsibility for their abusive behavior often make separation difficult for the victim in a number of ways. Some of the most common behaviors include inappropriate discussions with people outside the relationship; continued, unwanted contact with the victim, financial irresponsibility and abuse.

Telling others intimate information about the victim or spreading lies or rumors are signs of an abuser who will not reform. An abuser may believe that ruining the reputation of the victim or turning friends and family against her will force the victim to take the abuser back. In reality, it should have the opposite effect: such mean behavior is a warning that the abuse will continue.

Continuing to talk to others as if the marriage is still intact or there is hope for reconciliation can also be controlling. It may be an indication that the abuser does not grasp the seriousness of the situation. In addition, it may cause others to minimize the problem and pressure the victim to get over it.

Some abusers continue to communicate with the victim directly or through others even when ordered not to. Sending e-mails, calling, having others call or send messages and showing up at the place of employment constitute harassment and continued abuse. If the abuser was the one to move out, he or she no longer has the right to be at the family home once separation has occurred without possible legal consequences. Utilizing the children to communicate messages to the other parent is exceptionally abusive and demonstrative of a lack of concern and love for the children. Passing messages through the children in this way places the children in the middle of the adults' issues. If this occurs, it should be documented and shared with the victim's attorney and therapist and the police.

Many abusers use money to control their victims. Some believe that if they are not living in the family home, they do not need to continue to pay the mortgage or that if they are not allowed contact with the children, they do not have to make child support payments. The bottom line is that the abuser is legally and morally required to maintain all ordered or agreed-upon payments. An abuser may also have the false belief that the victim will have to accept the abuser's financial debts. The reality is that whatever debts the abuser accrues after separation will be his own. An attorney can help protect the victim in this situation.

The victim needs to recognize that if the abuser behaves in harmful, controlling ways even during separation, she is communicating clearly that she is not willing to cease the abusive behavior. In such cases divorce may be appropriate.

Even if the abuser abides by standards of appropriate behavior during the separation, both parties need to consider if and how they wish to proceed. If you are separated from your partner, take this opportunity to evaluate the relationship. This may help you decide whether divorce is the right choice for you. It will also help you prepare for the future, either with the same partner or in another relationship. Without resolving the issues that contributed to the current situation, you are more likely to continue the same problems in future relationships. Appendix VII provides a worksheet to help you take stock of your relationship. If possible, you should also have your spouse complete a copy of this worksheet so you can discuss your answers; however, it will be a valuable tool even if you use it alone.

Separation is an important first step for divorce. Both parties begin pulling back the energy they had invested in the marriage and in the other partner. This change is necessary for a successful divorce and requires that limits be set and enforced.

If the couple has children, both partners need to prepare for single parenting. The primary custodial parent will take on new responsibilities and begin to make most decisions pertaining to the home and children. The children will experience their own difficulties with this new arrangement. These need to be addressed. Remember, however, that it is always far healthier for children to come from a divorced home than to live in an abusive home.

Divorce

The divorce process is a lengthy one. Typically, a divorce takes about six months at the very least. It is emotionally draining and a time of sorrow. Allocating time during the divorce process for your children, your family and yourself is imperative. To remain grounded and well balanced, keep the following guidelines in mind.

Be realistic in setting time aside for paperwork, problem identification and meetings with your attorney. Avoid beginning new projects that are unnecessary. Taking on too much only serves to spread your time and energy more thinly. While you may wish to find things to do to distract yourself from the thoughts and stressors of the divorce process, remember that distraction offers only temporary relief and often makes the process harder. Instead, set aside and prioritize time for self-reflection, support and rest.

Maintain relationships with family, friends, church contacts and your psychologist or mediator. Divorce is not something to take on without the ongoing support of others.

Take care of your own physical needs, including sleep, nutrition and exercise. Sleep and nutrition are necessary to maintain physical and emotional health. Exercise not only will help with stress reduction, but will provide you a break from problems while you engage in healthy behavior. Avoid the use of alcohol.

Allocate time to prepare for divorce mentally and emotionally. One of the realities of divorce is that it brings about many significant changes. Examine the expected and possible changes as early in the divorce process as possible. List both positive and negative changes, being realistic. Take time to develop a plan to address the negative changes. Frequently review the list of positive changes to provide yourself strength and motivation.

Journal your experiences. It really does help. I recommend using an outline, bullet format rather than sentences or paragraphs. It is easier to reflect on your journal entries at a later time when they are written in a summarized fashion.

Remember that your children need you in their lives even more during divorce. They need your time and investment, as well as your reassurance that things will work out. Maintain routines, activities and special celebrations as you normally would. This will go a long way to helping your children as well as you in the healing process. Engage relatives to assist with child-care and visitation to increase your children's support network.

Maintain appropriate boundaries with your children. Always conduct divorce business outside of their presence. To involve your children directly in the divorce process is nothing short of abuse. There are some topics on which it may be appropriate to obtain your children's opinions and preferences; however, they are not in a position or developmentally capable to make the final decision.

If one partner has been abusive, then no visitation with the other partner or the children should occur outside structured, supervised settings. Utilize public meeting places to discuss divorce issues. You and your children should never be put into a situation where your physical, sexual or emotional well-being or safety is in jeopardy. This should remain the rule of thumb until the abuser has been involved in a treatment program to address abuse and a psychologist has determined that he or she is no longer a significant threat to the safety of anyone.

In addition, the victim of abuse should complete his or her own healing process before any contact occurs with the abuser. Even then, a qualified professional, not a family member, should supervise the contact. The victim's rights to safety supercede the abuser's right to contact with his or her children or partner. Following these recommendations will protect everyone from ongoing abuse.

Remember that approximately 80 percent of abusive relationships end and most abusive marriages do not survive. Understand that the abuser must be willing to cease all abusive behavior—not only the physical abuse, but the controlling behavior, sarcasm and other verbal abuse as well. Many abusers are simply not ready or willing to sacrifice their power and control.

Remember that the goal is to divorce in the least destructive manner possible; it is not in your best interest or that of your partner to make the process any more difficult than it has to be. Follow these general rules to make the process more tolerable for both of you.

1. Treat your partner with respect. You may be angry and hurt, but nothing will be accomplished without respect.
2. Avoid complaining about your partner to family, friends, neighbors, coworkers and children. Discussing your problems with those involved in your support network is one thing, but to only complain adds stress to the situation. Do not slander your partner. Talk only about the facts; do not embellish. Take responsibility for any role you played in the problems.
3. Do not engage in abusive or controlling behavior.
4. Establish a plan to use time-outs if the situation with your partner becomes abusive or unproductive.
5. Allow time for you and your partner to process and deal with problems and discussions. Know when to stop a discussion.
6. Utilize professionals to help guide the divorce process. In addition to an attorney, a therapist or mediator can offer added support and guidance to both you and your children. This can often result in a more agreeable and fair outcome for everyone.

Divorce can be a healthy and healing choice. Take the time to heal and keep a positive mindset. When in doubt about anything, consult a psychologist, mediator or attorney.

CHAPTER 16

Grief and Relationship Violence

Both victims and abusers of domestic and dating violence experience a sense of loss. With this come feelings of grief and bereavement. The sudden change of a relationship can at times seem devastating. Abuse changes everything. The dream of having a loving and caring relationship and the dream of living happily ever after with your partner have been lost.

Grief is defined as the normal reaction to a loss expressed through emotions and behaviors. *Bereavement* refers to an internal realization of an external reality and includes loss and mourning; this means that the person realizes and is aware of what has happened. *Loss* refers to a perceived or actual loss, including the loss of a significant other, of rights (being violated), of an object or of morals, values or dreams. *Mourning* refers to the process of adapting to loss. The mourning process occurs along with bereavement.

How Grief Is Experienced

Grief may take many forms, including a state of shock or numbness, general confusion, disturbance of appetite or sleeping patterns, impaired concentration, preoccupation with the lost object or person and a withdrawal from others and activities. As a result of the ways in which grief may be experienced and expressed, it is easy to understand how grief can often be mistaken for other problems such as depression, eating disorders or alcohol and drug abuse. Despite the fact that grief shares many characteristics and symptoms with these other problems, there are differences between them.

Grief differs from depression in that the mood swings during grief tend to occur within a short time span and are typically from sad to normal. With depression, however, the mood swings tend to last longer. A person suffering from grief will also become increasingly interested in others and activities as the individual copes with the grief, whereas with depression the person's interest in others and activities usually does not improve until the depression subsides or until therapy is sought. A person experiencing grief usually focuses guilt on what was done or not done in relation to the lost person, whereas with depression the person usually experiences shame rather than guilt. This shame is usually focused on the person's own self-worth and the person therefore may believe that he is bad or worthless.

Other problems may exist along with grief and when appropriate several problems may be addressed in therapy simultaneously. However, it is imperative to accurately identify and separate which issues are grief and which are indicative of more serious problems, remembering that grief is a normal reaction to loss.

Nevertheless, it is important to deal with grief and loss issues so that they do not continue to impact a victim's or abuser's life. When grief issues are not adequately dealt with, the problems associated with grief may continue for years, resulting in long-term resentment, anger confusion, fear of abandonment and lack of trust. To resolve grief issues, one must accept and properly identify the grief and, if necessary, seek therapy to help adjust to the loss and to overcome the problems associated with grief.

How a person experiences the bereavement process is related to that person's level of development, past and present experiences, future expectations and social stressors. Some people may attempt to avoid dealing with loss, as if all of the feelings and other investments surrounding the lost person will just disappear over time. For example, many adults truly believe that if they terminate an abusive relationship, they will somehow forget about it. This only leads to unresolved grief. Memories are never forgotten; a person either deals with them or buries them. If they are buried, they will resurface and create further and deeper problems in the future.

Loss affects a person's life in six areas:

1. *Physical Effects*: nightmares, disturbance of appetite and/or sleep patterns, lethargy (lack of energy, hopelessness, etc.), heavy or tight chest, body aches and restlessness.

2. *Cognitive Effects*: difficulty with concentration; constant thoughts of the lost person, object, rights, safety or dreams (includes actual, expected or perceived loss); daydreams and nightmares.

3. *Emotional Effects*: sadness, anger, guilt, shame, loneliness, fatigue, numbness, suicidal thoughts and depression.

4. *Behavioral Effects*: sleep disturbance (difficulty falling or remaining asleep); appetite disturbance (loss of appetite, binge-purging or overeating); crying; social withdrawal; avoidance of reminders of lost person, object, dream or moral; acting out sexually; alcohol and/or drug abuse.

5. *Spiritual Effects*: doubts of a higher power, thoughts of deserving loss as a form of punishment.

6. *Relationship Effects*: decreased communication, decreased desire for intimacy, loss of pleasure from or attraction to significant other, loneliness and emptiness and boredom or fear of relationships.

The Five Stages of Grief

Most people go through five stages of grief. These are

1. **Denial** A grieving person's mind wants to protect him or her from the pain, so she may deny that any problem exists. At this time, the mind decides that the griever is not ready mentally,

emotionally or spiritually to address or handle the loss. The more an individual has depended on the lost object or person, the stronger the denial. Abuse takes a heavy toll because the victim has invested a lot of time, energy and emotion in the relationship with the abuser. A person in denial will often try to isolate herself. She is likely to feel powerless.

2. **Anger** Both victims and abusers may feel angry over the loss of a relationship and the damage to hopes and dreams. Victims may be angry over the loss of the sense of security in the relationship. A person in this stage begins to experience regrets. He may express anger in destructive ways (e.g., demonstrating rage or violent behavior) or turn it inward against himself (e.g., depression, suicide). It is in this stage that a person experiences disappointment with the self and sometimes a sense of self-hatred.

3. **Bargaining** In this stage the victim attempts to postpone the inevitable and to control the uncontrollable. She bargains with God, family, friends or even the abuser. This is another attempt to avoid facing reality.

4. **Depression** Sorrow, despair and a great sense of sadness occur. Anger turns within, becoming self-destructive. Grieving victims may experience mild to severe depression and may need psychological intervention. They may find themselves crying uncontrollably. This stage is temporary and necessary.

5. **Acceptance** The final stage of grieving is the resolution of grief. The victim accepts that the abuser was in fact abusive and that the victim did not deserve to be abused or make the abuser abuse. A person in this stage begins to see hope instead of gloom, power instead of powerlessness.

Although all people go through these stages when experiencing loss, they may experience them in different orders and may find themselves revisiting some of the stages on occasion. This is normal and part of the individual healing process.

Relationships are also affected by loss in many ways. According to Erickson, some of the common effects include

- inability to attain genuine intimacy
- enmeshment (losing oneself in the other, becoming one with the other) or disengagement (distancing from the other, no investment of energy in the relationship or the other person)
- over-dependence on each other
- anger used as the main method of communication
- increase in conflicts and power struggles
- one person doing the feeling for both
- strained sexual relationship
- problems in other relationships (family, friends, etc.)

Any combination of these can strain a relationship and the result may be a loss of a healthy relationship, of friends or of a sense of sanity.

The Mourning Process

Once loss occurs, grieving must occur to restore equilibrium and complete the mourning process. Just as a child needs to complete certain tasks for growth and development to occur, adults must also complete the mourning process so as not to impair their own growth and development. According to J. M. Worden, author of *Grief Counseling and Grief Therapy*, mourning involves four steps.

Step 1, whether you are a victim or an abuser, is to accept the reality of the loss. Loss of a loved one due to death, while painful, is more straightforward, in that the person is forever gone. When a relationship ends, the task of grieving is made more difficult by the fact that the person is still around. In certain situations, such as when a couple has children, a victim may never be fully able to terminate all contact with the abuser. However, abuse does cause loss, including that of a significant other, of safety or of dreams.

During this step you must overcome the defense of denying that the loss has occurred. It is important that you accept the reality that you were abused or that you have abused your significant other. Often victims will acknowledge that they were abused by a significant other but will minimize and deny the effects and severity of the abuse. Abusers also tend to minimize their abusiveness or the effects of their abuse. But minimizing and denying the actual experience of being abused only serves to cheat you of your right to heal. If you cannot fully accept and appropriately label the violence as abuse, the healing process will be severely hampered or may not occur at all.

Step 2 is to fully experience the pain of grief. The importance of experiencing this pain cannot be overstated. Experiencing dating violence is hurtful and it can be difficult to allow yourself to accept the hurt. Alcohol, drugs, denial and avoidance all aid in burying the pain. Yet the pain exists regardless of whether or not you choose to feel it. If delayed, the pain will be harder to deal with and may complicate your life by creating other problems that prevent you from completing the grieving process. To deny the pain only serves to cheat yourself of healing. Acknowledge that it is okay to feel bad from time to time and to talk about those feelings. Allow yourself to feel sad, depressed or disappointed sometimes. You can handle these negative emotions and they do not dictate your worth.

Remembering some pleasant and caring moments is normal. Most abusers have some positive qualities, which may have been particularly noticeable at the start of the relationship. It is important that you not devalue positive memories; they may hold a special place in your heart and may explain why you cared for the abuser. Give yourself permission to enjoy them, but give yourself permission to experience the negative emotions as well.

Step 3 is to adjust to an environment, relationship and significant other that are not abusive. It is important to develop new skills you can use to accomplish the tasks that your significant other once did for you. For example, the abuser may have fulfilled the role of sexual partner, accountant and decision maker. Now you need to learn how to accomplish these and other tasks without him or her.

Step 4 is to withdraw emotional energy and reinvest it in another relationship. Refocus emotional energy into new relationships and allow yourself to love again. Self-identity, individualization and self-love are often lost when abuse occurs, especially when abuse occurs over a long period of time. The goal is to learn about yourself, to focus on yourself and to expand and enhance friendships for support. This does not mean to forget about the other person, but rather to invest energy in other relationships.

Although it can be awkward, frightening and challenging to experience a relationship based on trust, respect and love rather than paranoia, fear and violence, reinvesting emotional energy into a nonabusive dating relationship can be emotionally rewarding for a victim. Life offers no guarantees. However, if you have healed from the abuse, you will be more likely to find healthy people with whom to spend time. Abusers who experience their own pain learn to deal with problems in healthy ways, allowing them to feel whole again as well.

Effects of Society on Individual Development and Loss

Society teaches men and women how to behave by setting certain expectations. Culturally, men are often taught to be leaders, to achieve and to be in control. Men are often taught at a young age not to cry, not to show emotions and not to be submissive in relationships. What is lost here is a very vital aspect of any person: the license to show loving, caring, gentle feelings. But this is not all; for example, the dream of experiencing a relationship based on trust, respect and love is lost when abuse occurs.

Women are often taught to be submissive, to give care and to be obedient. In an article in the journal *Women and Therapy*, S. Smith reports that as a result of such values and teachings of society, being abused may be a consequence of or part of female development. Some of the losses experienced by women include the loss of freedom, individuality, intimacy and dreams. Many women also give up the power to express themselves freely, to have their own needs met (because of the expectation that they should give care) and to have control and ownership of their bodies.

Although these are often thought of as old standards, they are very much alive today, especially within some religious communities and cultures. In some cultures there still exists a misbelief that it is all right for a man to physically, sexually and verbally abuse his wife. This has carried over into the dating relationship and, as a result, dating violence occurs. In their article "The nature and antecedents of violent events," Dobash and Dobash found that most violent acts begin with a verbal confrontation, followed by attempts by women to avoid violence and finally the physical attack. A sense of safety and security, as well as peace of mind, is lost. There is a dwindling sense of power as the victim's attempts to defuse the violence fail. This example indicates the loss of power and control the victim experiences from both the abusive situation and the abuser. Both men and women may experience any of these losses.

Unfortunately, there are large information gaps pertaining to the issues of loss and grief. Further research into this area is needed. I believe that victims and abusers experience continued loss and that this loss is rarely identified or validated. The result is that the mourning process is rarely completed and therefore grief is ignored. Professionals need to see that both victims and perpetrators of abuse must learn to deal with the resulting issues of loss if they are to become part of healthy relationships in the future.

CHAPTER 17

Healing from Relationship Violence

When dating violence has occurred, it is imperative that the victim and abuser receive help so that they may recover from the effects of abuse. Many people believe that simply ending an abusive relationship will end their problems and that they will not be affected any longer once the relationship has ended. This will never work for abusers; it may work for some victims, but most victims will continue to experience problems in future relationships.

Reality has shown that abuse can affect a person's life physically, emotionally, cognitively, sexually and spiritually. It is important to remember that memories can never be forgotten or erased, no matter how hard a person tries. If an individual buries them, they will find some way to resurface later.

Some people believe that once a person is a victim or abuser, he or she will *always* be a victim or abuser. This is a myth. People can and do recover from the effects of abuse. The way most people get stuck, however, is by keeping the abuse a secret and refusing to receive help.

People maintain the secret of abuse when they accept the blame for their significant others' behavior. Most often it is the victim who does this, somehow believing that he is responsible for having been abused. But no one can ever cause a person to abuse another, just as a person can never cause someone to change. It is the *abuser's choice* to be violent and the *abuser's choice* to receive or not to receive help. Another way to keep abuse secret is to bury the problem by denial or by alcohol or drug use. The more a person runs away from a problem, however, the longer the person will remain trapped in the role of victim or abuser, because no one can heal until she openly chooses to deal with the problem.

Claim your circumstances instead of allowing them to claim you. Take responsibility for your choices and then make a decision about new behavior. Take control of your life on your terms.

The Healing Process

Ending a violent dating relationship involves several steps. The first step is to acknowledge the problem. No problem will go away by being ignored. Admit what is happening as honestly as possible. It is impossible to change when either person has not identified the problem.

Let us examine how each one can take this crucial step.

Accepting That Abuse Occurred
A Victim's Perspective

It is often difficult for a person to accept that he or she has been a victim. Accepting that one has been abused requires one to experience the impact of the abuse.

The promises often made in relationships provide a sense of security, respect and love. When most couples marry, they believe that they will be married for life, grow old together, raise the children together, live in their home together, be safe and take care of each other. Abuse shatters the dreams born of those promises. But eventually, the reality sinks in: you realize as you learn about abuse that you have been abused. Painful though it may be, acknowledging the abuse is a necessary step in the grieving process.

Victims can come to accept the reality of their experiences in several ways. Talking with friends, family and professionals can help if these people support and validate the victim's experience. Reading books on abuse may allow a victim to recognize her situation in examples and descriptions. In the end, the victim must allow herself to be vulnerable and accept that she has been abused, taken advantage of, hurt, belittled and injured.

The first time most people recognize themselves as victims, they get a sinking feeling in their stomachs. Disbelief and horror overcome some victims and it feels almost like a bad dream that cannot possibly be true. With time, however, a victim must realize that he has been abused.

It is at this point when a victim can begin to think about protecting him- or herself and the children from the abuser. If you are a victim, you need as much support and education as possible. Begin with these steps:

1. Seek out family members and friends who validate your experience by believing you.

2. Get involved with a battered women's support program. The staff of these programs can educate you about your rights and about healing and can guide you through the legal process. They provide trained advocates who will help you obtain orders for protection and will even go to court with you. These programs often have a good working relationship with the local police and courts, helping them to provide you with accurate information and protection. They can also help with temporary shelter when necessary. If you are a man who has been abused, you still may need to rely on a battered women's program for support, as there are very few resources specifically for men. However, the staffs of battered women's programs are usually trained to address the needs of male victims as well. No one there will put you down for seeking assistance.

3. Get involved in an abuse support group. The power of group experience is beyond comprehension. A therapist can offer emotional support and therapy, an attorney can provide legal assistance, but only a support group can offer the peace of mind and sanity that comes with the realization that you are not alone. I strongly encourage all of my clients to attend support groups and often verify that they are attending. Victims involved in a support group often heal much faster and have much more support and safety. For tips on choosing a support group, see the section on therapy options later in this chapter.

4. Find a therapist who specializes in working with abuse issues. Again, the end of this chapter has guidelines that will help you find the right professional for your situation.

5. Decide whether an order for protection is necessary. Orders for protection are court orders telling the abuser that he or she can have no contact with you. An order for protection is necessary when the abuser
   • refuses to leave the home
   • continues to threaten you or the children
   • harasses you in any way
   • has been physically abusive towards you or your children
   • has made any threats to seriously harm you, your children or him- or herself
   At times you may wonder if your situation is serious enough for an order for protection or whether you are being mean to the abuser if you obtain one. The reality is that if any of the above situations are present, then the risk for further serious harm is high and you need the protection of the court. If the abuser complies with the court order and seeks help, then the order for protection does not create any significant hardship for him or her. It is only when he or she refuses to comply with the order that the consequences become much more serious. Only the abuser can choose to comply or not. When

the court issues you an order for protection, they are telling you that your situation warrants such action. They are validating your experience and acknowledging the harm your abuser has caused and the threat that he or she still poses.

6. Find an attorney who specializes in abuse and family law. Many attorneys do not understand verbal and psychological abuse, so be patient. Have your therapist and battered women's advocate communicate with your attorney to make certain he or she understands your situation. If you have any concerns about what your attorney is advising, consult your therapist and advocate prior to making any final decisions, even if your attorney pressures you by telling you something must be decided or signed immediately. A competent attorney will not be offended by your consulting with others about decisions.

7. Obtain psychological support for your children as well. Even if they have not been directly abused, they have experienced the ramifications of the abuse. Most are more aware of the abuse than anyone would want to believe. Children who witness abuse are at far more risk for becoming abusers than other children. The impact of living in an abusive home is dramatic and affects all of the residents' lives forever.

An Abuser's Perspective

Abusers may have just as much difficulty recognizing and accepting that they have become abusers. Any act of abuse, no matter how minor, is a planned choice on the abuser's part. However, he or she may never have labeled these acts as abusive and may not fully realize he or she now fits the definition of "abuser."

For an abuser, addressing abuse requires accepting the fact that he has been the perpetrator of abuse. This first step in the long healing process is difficult and draining. However, it allows the abuser to obtain much-needed help and to learn not to be abusive. Even if one relationship is ending, the abuser needs to address the abusive behavior in order to prevent it from ruining future relationships.

Accepting that one has been the perpetrator of abuse requires experiencing the impact of one's behavior. Many abusers made promises that provided a sense of security, respect and love. Those who married vowed to be married for life and take care of each other in sickness and in health, just as the victims did. It is often difficult for an abuser to admit that she has broken these promises and shattered dreams of a loving relationship by abusing a partner. Eventually, however, the reality must sink in if any change is to occur.

Abusers realize the truth in several ways. Seeing themselves or their situation in examples in books on abuse can be helpful. Another important move is talking with friends, family or professionals who recognize the abuse for what it is. The most essential step is for the abuser to allow himself to be vulnerable and accept that he has been abusive and damaged trust, probably to such a degree that trust will never again occur within the relationship.

A person recognizing herself as an abuser may be overcome by disbelief and horror. He may experience an overwhelming sense of shame, guilt and embarrassment. What kind of person abuses those he or she loves? The truth is that love and abuse do not occur for long together; love quickly becomes replaced with a sense of ownership over the victim. The abuser may experience anger, frustration and irritation frequently and find it difficult to feel inner peace.

If you can recognize yourself as an abuser and are willing to invest in changing, you are ready to begin the healing process. Start by thinking about protecting your victim and your children from your abusive behavior. As you plan how to do this, you need as much support and education as possible. The following steps are a good way to begin:

1. Own full responsibility for your choice to engage in abusive behavior. Blaming your victim portrays an irrational and blatantly inaccurate picture to friends and family. Making excuses will only make changing more difficult: how can you alter a behavior if you refuse to believe that you control it?

2. Find support from family and friends who validate your experience by believing that you have been abusive. Do not allow others to provide justifications and excuses. Stand your ground. Accept the embarrassment and shame that come with owning your abusive behavior. You will usually find that others support you when you are honest.

3. Get involved with an anger management or abuse program. You will not be able to stop your abusive behavior on your own. Very few abusers change on their own; most end up abusing once again, destroying any sense of trust or hope for saving the relationship. You deserve support and counseling that focuses on your needs. Approach the program with an open mind. The staffs at these programs are trained to address anger management and abuse issues. No one there is going to put you down. They are concerned that you are open and willing to admit your problems, including your anger issues. Give the program a chance. Men in particular often find it difficult dealing with feelings and problem-solving skills at first, but quickly learn the benefit of becoming more genuine and empathetic.

4. Address alcohol and drug use separately from the anger management and anger treatment. Quite often abusers blame their chemical use for causing them to behave abusively. The reality is that alcohol and drug use simply serve as disinhibitors; that is, they make it easier to use the intoxicated state as an excuse for abuse.

5. If your victim has obtained an order for protection, then respect it and follow the limits set forth. First, it is a court order and any violation of it will result in criminal charges and likely incarceration. Second, if your victim is that afraid of you, then respect his or her experience and perception. You have no idea of the degree of harm caused to your victim, the terror and fear that simply do not go away.

The vast majority of abusers refuse to change and will remain abusive in all of their intimate relationships. Those who choose to cease their abusive behavior have several things in common: They are willing to accept full responsibility for their abusive behavior and have a sincere belief that they are at fault. In addition, they do not wait for the court or others to recommend treatment: they initiate treatment.

Step two in the healing process is admitting the responsibility for one's own actions. No one is perfect; we all make mistakes, but no mistake ever justifies being abusive. Put the blame where it belongs—with the abuser. The only person one can ever be responsible for is oneself. Taking back that power can be energizing and calming. If you are a victim, stop accepting responsibility for your abuser's behavior. It is important for the abuser to accept full responsibility for his or her violent behavior and stop rationalizing and justifying the abuse.

Step three is to restore the self-pride and self-esteem that abuse has taken away. Both victim and abuser lose self-esteem and pride when abuse occurs—the victim as a result of being degraded, abused and violated as a human being, and the abuser when she chooses to use violence against a significant other as a way to have needs met. Both the victim and abuser are capable of restoring their own pride and esteem.

Remember that this is not a passive process. If you are grieving from an abusive relationship, there are steps you can take to restore yourself. As you move through them, remember to reinforce your efforts and accomplishments. Give yourself rewards for every new task completed in your healing journey.

Restoring the Self
1. See yourself where you are today. Most victims begin in the "survival and denial" mode. This is existing, not living. Give yourself permission to heal and to move on. Begin to document, through journaling, your thoughts, feelings, accomplishments and attempts at healing. A record of your healing journey can be very rewarding. It is your story about your life.

Looking back after some time, seeing where you were a year ago and comparing it to where you are now is very satisfying.

2. Realize that you cannot change others. You are responsible for your own behavior and no one else's. By recognizing your limitations, you actually gain power from the knowledge that nothing you did caused the abuse.

3. Identify and work through personal issues. The goal is to better understand yourself. A major issue for many victims is dependence. If an abuser has forced you to be dependent upon him or her, you now have to address your fears associated with independent behavior. Before you were involved in a relationship with the abuser, you were independent. You can be independent again and be happy! Identify how dependent behaviors limit you in getting your own needs met and communicate mixed messages. Abusers interpret graciousness, compliance and caring behavior as an indication that abuse is acceptable. You have the power to be assertive and to communicate directly and effectively what you want. Take time to talk with friends, family members or a therapist to learn how to develop these skills.

4. *Reintegration* means learning to be okay with yourself. This prepares you to take care of yourself and get your own needs met. Identify your own competence and self-worth. You have always been competent in life, but you have allowed the abuser to make you feel incompetent. Abusers invest a lot of energy in making victims feel worthless and incompetent, because abusers actually feel inferior to their victims. If an abuser has taught you distorted ways of thinking about yourself, you will need to reestablish your sense of pride, value and esteem. Challenge your cognitive distortions and develop new, rational self-talk. Write the new self-talk down. Give yourself permission to say nice things about yourself.

5. Develop strategies for being alone for brief periods of time. Give yourself time to become comfortable with yourself.

Abusers usually isolate victims, straining relationships with family, friends and others. You have a right to have these relationships. Work to reestablish them. You may need time before entering another romantic or dating relationship. Some delay is natural and a good chance to reconnect with your children, family and friends. Being without a romantic partner helps you to become more grounded. When the time is right, you will find you have much more energy and satisfaction from the new relationship.

6. Embrace a new beginning. Living a new, emotionally healthy way of life is highly rewarding, although you will still face challenges. When difficulties arise, use reframing techniques: Always attempt to find alternate meanings to situations with which you are faced. There are usually several possible positive and negative interpretations, so take the time to explore them.

7. Remember the most important self-talk: "I have been through something like this before. I can do it again!" Look back through your journal. You now have the strength to stand up to the most difficult situations. You have faced similar stresses and complications and successfully addressed them. You are now ready for any of life's trials.

Step four of the healing process is to follow through with all commitments. For victims to learn how to break out of the victim role takes time and effort. Victims may remain in the victim role until they learn not to accept anything less than respectful, caring relationships. In most instances it is the abuser who fails to follow through on commitments. Most abusers who begin therapy do not continue long enough to benefit in the long run. For long-lasting change, both victim and abuser need to understand that change does not come easily. Learning not to abuse or be abused takes more than just a promise to change.

Therapy Options

For those motivated to change, there are several options for both abusers and victims to overcome their abuse experiences. The options include *support groups, individual therapy, group therapy* and *couples therapy.*

Support groups offer a safe environment to express emotions, share histories and receive support from others who have similar experiences. The goal of such groups is to provide information, encouragement and backing. This is accomplished by education about abuse and coping with abuse and through peer support. The goal of a support group is not to change behavior but to offer encouragement and support for changes that have been made or are in the process of being made. Usually members will be involved in individual or group therapy while in the support group.

I caution victims and abusers to avoid using any twelve-step support group for dealing with issues of abuse. Twelve-step groups are not designed to address issues other than those specified—chemical dependency, sexual addiction or eating disorders. In fact, these groups can often worsen an abuser's or victim's situation because of the helpless and powerless role people assume they are in. There is no proof that twelve-step groups are effective or helpful when dealing with abuse issues.

Support groups are most often facilitated by volunteers who have experienced abuse themselves. Most have received some training, although the amount and quality of training varies greatly. Participation in support groups usually lasts two to twelve months, although some people attend for years.

Individual therapy involves meeting with a therapist alone. The primary advantage is that the person can receive individualized attention and may also be able to deal with other issues as they occur. Individual therapy offers the chance to identify specific issues, prepares the person for other therapy (group, couples or family) and allows the opportunity to practice and improve communication skills and other new behaviors without others present.

Most often the therapist will have a master's degree or sometimes a Ph.D. in psychology or social work. I do not recommend entering into therapy with anyone unless he or she at least holds a master's degree and is licensed as a psychologist or clinical social worker; the issues surrounding dating and domestic violence are extremely complex and require a therapist trained in abuse issues and other mental health issues.

It may take three to twelve sessions before therapy appears to be working. At that point a client should be seeing changes and feeling supported. If not, the client may need to find a different therapist. The reasons a therapist may not be right for an individual include a client not being ready for therapy, the therapist's style not fitting or the therapist not having expertise in working with abuse issues. Individual therapy is most effective when group therapy is occurring as well.

Group therapy offers the opportunity, under the guidance of a qualified therapist, to share experiences with others who have also been involved in abusive relationships. There are separate groups for abusers and victims. The goal of group therapy is to change behavior through education, role-playing and in-depth processing of issues. The difference between support groups and group therapy is that support groups are not effective in changing behavior but do strengthen changes that occur in therapy. Group therapy works on changing behaviors with the guidance of a trained therapist, offering more structure than a support group.

Group therapy has the advantage of drawing on the experiences and knowledge of all of the group members. Change often occurs when a group member gains insight or changes his or her behavior. This change also affects the other group members, who were in part responsible for encouraging and supporting the changes that occurred.

When the group is cohesive and strong, everyone takes an active role in confronting, supporting and guiding the other members. All can offer feedback while remaining focused on their own issues. Group therapy is the treatment of choice for both victims and abusers of relationship violence. Much more change can take place within a shorter amount of time with group therapy.

Group therapy lasts approximately six to twenty-four months. The same rule of time applies here as stated before: if after three months you are not seeing some change or feeling helped, seek a different group. Again, individual and group therapy together are the most effective regimen for treating abuse issues.

Couples therapy offers the victim and the abuser who want to remain together a chance to heal together; it is a prerequisite to rebuilding the relationship. *However, for couples therapy to be safe and effective in abuse situations, it must not occur until both the victim and the abuser have completed their own individual and group therapies or are far enough along in their therapy to safely attend couples therapy.* Both the abuser and the victim should be encouraged to continue in their support groups. If couples therapy is begun before both have completed their own healing processes, abuse is likely to continue or resume. This is because the couple is not ready openly to discuss their issues until they have identified their issues, have taken responsibility for their behaviors, have significantly modified their problem behaviors and are willing to deal calmly with these issues. In most cases, couples terminate their relationships before therapy has begun, mostly due to the lack of trust and the difficulty of guaranteeing the safety of the victim. Successful couples therapy may last approximately three to twelve sessions.

Individual and group therapy, as well as support groups, should be focused on the short term. Remember that a person who chooses to terminate therapy or support groups may return at a later time. I believe that people who experience abuse need time away from the support group and therapy to find out what has worked, what they have learned and what else they would like to change. They can then decide if they need further help to accomplish their goals or whether they can fulfill them on their own.

Unfortunately, if a victim remains involved in a support group or therapy longer than necessary, the group and therapy may revictimize him. Many group facilitators and therapists keep people involved in therapy or support groups longer than clinically necessary and as a result prevent them from making the changes the clients wanted or needed to make. This occurs when the therapist or facilitator begins to become a caretaker for the person treated, overprotects her or becomes over-empathetic, or when the therapist dislikes the client. Such an impasse can be identified when the therapist or facilitator refuses to let the client move on into the next phase of therapy or refuses to support the person's decision to terminate therapy. When any of these situations occur or when an abuser or victim is not encouraged to take risks or to practice new behavior changes, it is imperative that the client terminate therapy with that therapist.

One last problem that can occur is when the therapist or facilitator becomes friends with the victim or abuser, stepping out of the professional role into a more casual, social role. The reality is that once the therapist or facilitator has worked with a person in a professional role, whether in a support group or therapy setting, there should never be a social relationship with the client. Professional, ethical and legal guidelines prohibit this conduct and refer to this as a *dual relationship*.

Social and romantic relationships are not allowed because of the power that the therapist or counselor has over the client, as well as the fact that when the two met, the abuser or victim was vulnerable. If such contact occurs or is asked for or hinted at by the professional, the client should report the therapist to the psychology or social work licensing board or the state attorney general's office. If this professional is harming one person, he or she is probably harming other clients as well.

The primary goal for victims is to learn that they are not at fault for the abuse—it was the abuser's fault. Rebuilding the victim's self-esteem and confidence is the next step. The victim has the power to remain in or leave an abusive relationship. It is the victim's choice and it is imperative that he gain this understanding and self-empowerment. If the victim chooses to remain in an abusive relationship, however, in no way does it justify the person being victimized or place the blame on the victim. In therapy, victims become aware that they have the power to make decisions. It is not always possible to prevent an abusive incident from happening, but knowing what to do if it does happen gives the victim power to protect herself from further abuse and offers the opportunity to take legal action against the abuser. The final step is learning not to allow others to abuse one and how to protect oneself should it happen again. The best protection is prevention and this includes the protection plan in Appendix IV.

The primary goals for abusers are to learn what constitutes abuse and to stop abusing their victims and others. It is important for abusers to pay special attention to their cue areas so that they will know when they are escalating. When escalation occurs, abusers can choose to remove themselves from the situation and release their tension by exercising, meditating or performing some other activity.

In order to move on, abusers must accept that they are 100 percent responsible for their abusive behaviors and that no one ever causes them to behave violently. Understanding that provocation does not cause or justify violence is extremely important. Learning and believing that there are no excuses for the occurrence of violence is essential. Violence is always a choice and the abuser is always in control.

If an abuser is going to change his or her abusive tendencies permanently, a commitment to change must occur. This involves a significant amount of work, patience and risk. The abuser may also have other serious problems, such as mental illness or alcohol or drug dependency, that may require additional treatment.

One of the hardest things for an abuser to do is to find support groups to attend. Most support groups are for victims only. Yet support groups can be valuable for abusers, too. If a formal support group for abusers is not available, it may be necessary to find another type of support group to attend. Without ongoing support for at least six to twelve months after the completion of therapy, the victim and abuser may find it difficult to maintain their behavior changes. This lack of support does not in any way justify abuse recurring, but rather places an extra burden on the abuser to find an appropriate support network.

Only qualified mental health professionals can offer the appropriate help to allow both victim and abuser to recover from an abusive personal relationship. Because abuse always becomes increasingly violent over time, it is imperative that both victim and abuser receive the help they need.

The negative effect of people failing to complete therapy is that they may believe that the other person—not them—had problems and that they do not have to make any changes. However, both victims and abusers need to change. If people do not take care of the underlying issues of abuse, but only deal with the symptoms, the problem of abuse will perpetuate itself.

Appendices

CHARACTERISTICS OF ABUSERS

1. May have intense, dependent relationships with their victims.
2. May be jealous and possessive of their significant others.
3. Lose temper easily, often overreacting.
4. May be generally impulsive.
5. Tend to minimize and deny that they have problems with violence.
6. Behave violently toward significant others.
7. Experience difficulty identifying and expressing emotions other than jealousy, anger and hostility.
8. May behave violently toward others, pets or objects.
9. May abuse alcohol and/or drugs and may use this to justify their violence.
10. May have dual personality ("Jekyll and Hyde").
11. May have been abused themselves or observed others being abused.
12. Rigid and dichotomous thinking.
13. Expect their significant others to spend most or all free time with them and to report where they have been.

14. May have stereotypical ideas of how men and women should act.
15. Extremes in behaviors and moods (quick to anger, overdoes nice things, overly cruel, etc.).
16. May have many friends, be well liked by others and may even have special talents.
17. May use weapons for protection or to abuse others.

Appendix II

CHARACTERISTICS OF VICTIMS

1. May fear significant others' tempers.
2. May attempt to avoid conflicts and disagreements at any cost.
3. Changes in behaviors, becoming increasingly withdrawn, aggressive or vigilant of significant others' presence.
4. Changes in mood, becoming increasingly depressed, anxious, irritable or even angry.
5. May experience disrupted eating or sleeping patterns.
6. May use and abuse drugs or alcohol in an attempt to numb reality of having been abused.
7. May have poor self-esteem and self-image.
8. May have physical injuries evidenced by marks, scars and bruises.
9. May behave differently around their significant others than around friends, co-workers and family members.
10. May have disrupted concentration.
11. May avoid friends or terminate relationships.
12. May have suicidal thoughts or may have attempted suicide.
13. May have self-mutilations, such as cutting or burning.
14. May exhibit extremes in behavior, such as promiscuity, prostitution, stealing and reckless behavior.
15. May avoid discussing their relationships or abusers.
16. May take the blame for abuse.
17. May spend all free time with their significant others/abusers.
18. May insist on getting permission from their significant others before making any plans.
19. May experience headaches, nausea and other stress-related physical problems.

Appendix III

CHARACTERISTICS OF AN ABUSIVE RELATIONSHIP

1. The couple may avoid being around others, often staying home or going out alone rather than in groups.
2. One person appears to do the decision making for both people.
3. Both people may avoid discussing how the relationship is going or may focus only on the good qualities, avoiding discussing problem areas.
4. One person may be a scapegoat and blamed for causing all of the problems.
5. Abuse such as yelling and name calling may be open.
6. Marks or bruises may be noticed on one person.
7. One person may exhibit jealousy toward the other or may accuse the other of infidelity.
8. The couple openly experiences intense and sometimes violent arguments.
9. One person attempts to isolate the other from others and may even sabotage friendships to prevent the significant other from receiving support.
10. One person may be quiet and not call attention to self unless told to do so by the significant other.
11. Communication appears unhealthy, ineffective and one-sided.
12. One person may begin to do something that the other person clearly does not want to do, such as engaging in sexual behavior.

Appendix IV

VICTIM'S PROTECTION PLAN

During times of crisis it is often difficult to concentrate and all available options for self-protection may not be obvious. A protection plan allows the victim to follow a set of instructions that allow for maximum safety. Before the next crisis, write out the details of your plan using the following outline as a starting point.

1. Prearrange a place to go that is safe. This may be with friends, relatives or even a hotel.
2. Have the following packed and in a place that is accessible, such as in the car, closet, at work or with friends:
   • Clothes
   • Money, checkbook, charge cards
   • Important papers such as restraining orders, orders for protection, birth certificate, etc.
   • Phone numbers of friends, shelters, counselors, etc., along with a cellular phone if you own one.
3. Learn and understand the cues of escalation, signs of impending abuse, etc.
4. Find places where you can go when your partner is escalating.
5. Utilize "911" when abuse appears imminent. If you believe that you or your children are going to be abused, call "911" and get out of the house.
6. Tell friends, family and others about abuse to increase your support network. Remember, it is not your fault your partner chooses to abuse you.

If the protection plan is put in writing, it will be easier to follow during times of crisis. It is also important to pay attention to the abuser's cues, as explained in Chapter 3. When any of these cues are present, it is advisable to leave the situation if possible. It is of no use to discuss problems with someone who is escalating; he or she will only hear what he or she wants to hear.

Appendix V

DE-ESCALATION STRATEGIES
The following are suggestions of what to do if you find yourself
escalating. This is not an exhaustive list. You are encouraged to add
any of your own ideas.
 1. Take a time-out and leave the situation.
 2. Take a deep, gut breath. Hold it for a short time and slowly let
    it out. Take as many breaths as necessary.
 3. Tell yourself to calm down; hear yourself say it; listen to your-
    self.
 4. Call someone to talk with: a friend, relative, clergy member or
    other support person.
 5. Take a bath or shower.
 6. Write in a journal about the situation, your feelings, thoughts,
    etc.
 7. Exercise. However, do not engage in violent activities, such as
    martial arts, boxing or any other sport that involves or supports
    striking another person. Do not hit anything to vent. Sit-ups
    and push-ups are easily done anywhere!
 8. Contact your therapist.
 9. Contact a crisis line.
10. Reassure yourself that you have dealt appropriately with simi-
    lar situations and that you can choose a nonviolent and healthy
    response. Recall positive self-talk you have used in the past to
    calm down.
11. Stay focused on your goals. These may include remaining in
    your marriage, avoiding imprisonment or any other objective
    that is incompatible with escalation.
12. Do stretching exercises.
13. Go for a walk or run.
14. Go to a safe and relaxing place, such as a park, lake or health
    club.
15. Count to 10 or 100.
16. Utilize reframing techniques: listen to what your partner may
    be trying to say and try to hear other messages rather than
    focusing only on a negative perceived message.

17. Sit down. Do not stand over someone when angry. Try to be at eye level.
18. Listen to relaxing music. Have music that helps you to relax available.
19. Take responsibility for your role in the conflict.
20. Begin statements with "I"; own your statements and feelings.
21. Utilize notes to help remind yourself of what you should do. Put them everywhere!
22. Distract yourself with other activities (e.g., work, cleaning the house, garage or car, bird watching, being outdoors). Do not engage in activities that require full attention, such as using power tools.
23. Utilize relaxation techniques.
24. Empathize with your partner. Take time to accept responsibility for your role in the conflict and appreciate his or her perspective.
25. Visualize being in a calm, relaxing place.
26. Visualize solving the conflict in an appropriate manner.
27. Play with or groom your pet.
28. Slow down and smell the roses! Take time to notice and appreciate all of the good things in your life.
29. Remember the consequences from past occasions when you chose abusive or violent behavior; imagine these consequences occurring again if you choose not to cease your violent or abusive behavior now.
30. Attend a support group.
31. Choose your battles carefully and have a realistic, nonabusive strategy in mind before acting.
32. Pray or go to a religious service.

Things to Avoid
1. Getting the last word in or retaliating remarks
2. Driving
3. Drinking or drug use
4. Stress-producing activities (e.g., sports or other activities that involve competitive behavior, projects that require concentration or that are especially stressful)

5. Stewing about the problem or conflict
6. Blaming your partner and failing to take responsibility for your role in the conflict or problem
7. Rushing or pressuring your partner to discuss the problem
8. Discussing the problem with others and only presenting one side of the problem, seeking support for your point of view rather than an objective point of view
9. Failing to take prescription medication as directed
10. "Venting" by destroying property
11. Forcing or pressuring family and friends to take sides

Appendix VI

RELATIONSHIP RIGHTS

1. I have the right to refuse a date without feeling guilty.
2. I have the right to ask for a date without being crushed if the answer is no.
3. I have the right to choose to go somewhere alone without having to pair up with someone.
4. I have the right not to act macho or seductive.
5. I have the right to say no to physical closeness.
6. I have the right to say, "I want to know you better before I become more involved or before we have sex."
7. I have the right to say, "I don't want to be in this relationship any longer."
8. I have the right to an equal relationship with the opposite sex.
9. I have the right not to be abused physically, sexually or emotionally.
10. I have the right to change my life goals whenever I want.
11. I have the right to have friends, including those of the opposite sex.
12. I have the right to express my feelings.
13. I have the right to set limits, to say yes or no and to change my mind if I so choose, without permission from anyone else.
14. I have the right to stop doing something, even in the middle of it.
15. I have the right to have my morals, values and beliefs respected.
16. I have the right to say "I love you" without having sex.
17. I have the right to be myself, even if it is different from the norm or from what someone else wants me to be.
18. I have the right to say, "I don't want to please you at this time."
19. I have the right to talk with others about my relationships.
20. I have the right to be as open or as closed as I feel comfortable being.

Appendix VII:

EVALUATING A RELATIONSHIP
DURING SEPARATION

If you have separated from your significant other due to abuse, now is the time to evaluate the relationship. This will not only help you decide whether this relationship can continue; it will also help you avoid the same pitfalls in any future relationships. Take the time to examine your relationship carefully and closely and respect yourself enough to resolve the problems that you find. Remember, it is nearly impossible to resolve issues when you have not clearly identified what the issues are and what your role was in them.

Step One: Identify Issues That Were Problematic In…

A. The Relationship
Take the time to reflect upon the relationship. Be as specific as possible.
1. What have been the major problems?
2. At what point in the relationship did these problems occur and for how long?
3. What are the strengths of the relationship? Identify the strengths at the beginning, the middle and towards the end of the relationship. Which strengths remained and which disappeared or significantly lessened?
4. How has social behavior been integrated with the relationship? Has socializing with others interfered with spending time with your partner? Have you isolated yourselves, avoiding interaction with anyone but each other?
5. Have alcohol or drugs played a significant role in the relationship problems?
6. What problems or concerns, if any, have others identified about your relationship?

B. Your Partner

Without being vindictive or blaming, consider what your partner's role or responsibility has been in the relationship problems.

1. Identify the problems or issues that you believe your partner to have.
2. What has your partner done that you find irritating?
3. What do you wish that your partner had done that he or she chose not to?
4. Has your partner been abusive or controlling? If so, in what specific ways?
5. Has your partner abused alcohol or drugs while involved in the relationship?
6. Has your partner spent quality time with you or avoided alone time with you?

C. Yourself

To lessen your defensiveness, remember that the goal of this exercise is to identify issues and problems that you hope to change to allow yourself to engage in healthy relationships. You have the power to change your behavior and beliefs to improve your relationships and promote inner peace.

1. What have you said or done that has created problems in your relationship or with your partner?
2. What behavior have you engaged in that your partner finds irritating?
3. What have you failed to do that you know he or she wishes you had done?
4. Were you abusive or controlling? If so, in what specific ways?
5. Have you abused alcohol or drugs while involved in the relationship?
6. Have you spent quality time with your partner or avoided alone time with him or her?
7. What problems does your partner claim you have?

Step Two: In the Beginning...
Look back at the start of your relationship. Remember when you first met your partner, the excitement you felt and how attractive, sexy and interesting you found him or her to be. With those memories in mind, answer these questions
   1. What initially attracted you to your partner?
   2. What did your partner do or say that interested you?
   3. What was it about your partner's looks that attracted you?
   4. How did your partner make you laugh?
   5. How did your partner touch you that made you feel alive, excited, respected and cared for?
   6. What type of sexual behavior did you engage in that was meaningful and arousing to you?
   7. What made you want a relationship with this person?

Step Three: Timeline
Identify when the major problems arose. Place the problems on a timeline to help yourself gain a better understanding not only of when the problems began, but also for how long you both allowed the problems to worsen and the order of problems. Draw a line down a sheet of paper. On one side, describe each major event or problem in the relationship in the order that they occurred. On the other, write the approximate date of the problem. Use the sample on the next page as a guideline.

Step Four: Decision about Relationship
The next step is to decide whether the relationship can be saved. Answer the following questions.
   1. What will need to change to save this relationship?
   2. Am I willing and able to invest in the resolution process?
   3. Am I willing to do so in an open and respectful manner?
   4. Is my partner willing and able to invest in the resolution process?
   5. Is my partner willing to do so in an open and respectful manner?

September 2002	I met Melissa.
Fall-Winter 2002	I noticed that she seemed to contradict me often.
Spring 2003	Melissa started telling me that I don't know anything. I asked her to stop picking fights, but she said I enjoyed our "debates" as much as she did.
August 2003	I moved in with her.
December 2003	Melissa wanted me to go with her to New York when I had plans with my family. The day before, she told me if I really cared about her, I'd change my plans. I went to New York.
August 2004	Melissa called me at work so often my boss said something, so I asked her to cut back. She told me how mean I was being. I felt really guilty, so I tried to avoid her.
September 2004	I made a new friend. Melissa didn't like her and called her nasty names. I asked her not to and she accused me of wanting to have an affair. She said I would have to choose between them. I stopped talking to my new friend.
November 2004	I started looking for other places I could stay at night, because whenever I was home Melissa demanded to talk all the time. When I didn't voice opinions, she got mad; when I did, she said they were stupid. I felt stupid.
December 2004	Melissa got mad that I left a glass in the sink. She threw it at me. The next weekend I moved out.

If the answer to these questions is yes, then prioritize the problems and develop realistic strategies to accomplish the necessary changes. To do so will likely require that you engage in couples therapy rather than attempting it on your own. Having a third party involved who is neutral and skilled in relationship issues increases the chance that a resolution will occur and that the quality of the relationship will increase.

References

Barbaree, H. E., W. L. Marshall, and S. M. Hudson, eds. (1993). *The juvenile sex offender*. New York: Guilford Publications.

Bohmer, C. and A. Parrot (1993). *Sexual assault on campus: The problem and the solution*. New York: Lexington Books.

Corey, F. (1977). *Theory and practice of counseling and psychotherapy (2nd ed.)* Belmont, CA: Wadsworth.

Dobash, R.E., and Dobash, R.P. (1984). The nature and antecedents of violent events. *British Journal of Criminology*, 24. (From *Psychological Abstracts*, 1985, 72 (4), Abstract No. 14778).

Ellis, A., and Harper, R.A. (1975). *A new guide to rational living*. Englewood Cliffs, NJ: Prentice-Hall.

Erickson, B.M. (1986, Oct. 18). Clinical issues related to loss and bereavement. *St. Mary's College*, 11.

Fromm, E. (1956). *The art of loving*. New York: Harper & Row.

Harmon, R.J., Morgan, G.A., and Glicken, A.P. (1984). Continuities and discontinuities in affective and cognitive-motivational development. *Child Abuse and Neglect*, 8 (2), 156-167. (From *Psychological Abstracts*, 1985, 72 (7). Abstract No. 9106),

Hershorn, M., and Rosenbaum A. (1985). Children of marital violence: A closer look at the unintended victims. *American Journal of Orthopsychiatry*, 55 (2). (From *Psychological Abstracts*, 1985, 72 (7). Abstract No. 20395).

Johnson, S.A. (1992). *Man to man: When your partner says no.* Vermont: Safer Society Press.

Levy, B. (1984, May/June). Dating violence. *Networker.*

———. (1991). *Dating violence: Young women in danger.* Seattle, WA: Seal Press.

Makepeace, J. (1981, July/August). Premarital violence: Battering on college campuses. *Responses to Violence in the Family,* 4 (6).

Perez, C. (1993) "Stalking: When does obsession become a crime?" *American Journal of Criminal Law, 20,* 264-280.

Smith, S. (1984). The battered woman: A consequence of female development. *Women and Therapy,* 3(2), 3-9. (From *Psychological Abstracts,* 1985, 72 (4), Abstract No. 9808).

Swisher, K. L. and C. Wekesser (1994). *Violence against women.* Current Controversies. San Diego, CA : Greenhaven Press.

Valliere, V. N., and Lessig, R. (1995). "Relationships between alcohol use, alcohol expectancies, and sexual offenses in convicted sex offenders." Paper presented at the conference of the Association for the Treatment of Sexual Abusers, October 13.

Walen, S.R., DiGiusseppe, R., and Wessler, R.L. (1980). *A practitioner's guide to rational emotive therapy.* New York: Oxford University Press.

Walker, L. (1979). *The battered woman.* New York: Harper & Row.

Worden, J.M. (1982). *Grief counseling and grief therapy.* New York: Springer, pp. 7-17.

Index